DESIGN
D&T
MAKE IT!

textiles technology
for key stage 3

ALEX McARTHUR ■ TRISTRAM SHEPARD

First published in 2001 by:
Nelson Thornes Ltd
Delta Place
27 Bath Road
Cheltenham
GL53 7TH

02 03 04 05 / 9 8 7 6 5 4 3 2

A catalogue record of this book is available from the British Library.

ISBN 0 7487 4431 2

Designed and typeset by Carla Turchini
Picture research by John Bailey
Artwork by Tristram Ariss, Hardlines, Mike Gordon and Anna Roberts
Printed and bound in Italy by Canale

The authors would like to thank Rose Sinclair and Lesley Cresswell for their contributions as editorial consultants, Conrad Leach, and KIMM RARRAALL DESIGNS of Sawbridgeworth for providing information on Adinkra fabrics.

Where specific retailer's and manufacturer's products have been used to illustrate industrial practice they are not intended to imply any endorsement.

The publishers are grateful to the following for permission to reproduce photographs and other copyright material: 3M p.104; Acacia Adventure Holidays p.95; Adidas p.99; Admiral p.p. 114,115; Agfa p.75 (top); Ancient Art and Architecture Collection pp.12 (bottom left), 54 (centre left); Apple p.140; BASF p.44 (bottom); Bridgeman Art Library p.62 (Henri Matisse/Arts Council Collection/Hayward Gallery, London, UK); British Museum pp.30, 31 (Wellcome Collection); British Textiles Technology Group p.82; Brother UK p.107; Centre G. Pompidou p.53 (left – Helene Adant); Coats Viyella Home Furnishings pp.50, 51 (with thanks to Martin Coleman, Salford University and Alastair Grant, Jeff Joseph Technology College, Sale); Collections p.70 (top – Joanna Lewis); Crafts Council / Teresa Seattle pp.60 (left), 139 (top); David Hoffman Photolibrary p.75; Eye Ubiquitous pp.76 (top – Paul Seheult, bottom – David Cumming), 120 (David Cumming); Last Resort Picture Library p.45 (top); Martyn Chillmaid pp.13, 16, 28, 29, 40, 48, 49, 58, 68, 69, 91, 131; Oxfam p.15; Panos Pictures p.42 (Betty Press); Penn Nyla p.92; Petra Boase pp.56, 57, 60 (right); Robert Harding Picture Library p.83 (top – Adam Woolfitt); Science Photolibrary pp.80 (Rosenfeld Images Ltd), 93 (top), 132 (top – Deep Light Productions), 140 (top – Rosenfeld Images Ltd); Sony p.75 (bottom); Speedo p.99; Stockmarket pp.7 (bottom left), 106; Stone pp.22 (Will and Deni McIntyre), 46 (middle – Steven Weinberg); Succession H Matisse / DACS pp.52 (top right, bottom left), 53 (left); T K Mayy p.68; Tate Picture Library p.52 (right); Topham Picture Point p.54 (middle); Traidcraft pp.116 (right), 117 (bottom), 136, 137 (Zsa Zsa Soffe, Dezign Inc); Travelbag Adventures p.94; TRIP pp.45 (bottom – V Kolpakov), 121 (H Rogers); Tristram Shepard p.54 (top left); Umbro p.99; Victoria and Albert Museum p.122; W L Gore & Associates, Inc pp.100, 101, 143 (bottom).

Thanks to the staff and pupils of The Leys High School, Redditch for their help with the photography.

Every effort has been made to contact copyright holders. The publishers apologise to anyone whose rights have been overlooked and will be happy to rectify any errors or omissions at the earliest opportunity.

Contents

Introduction

Welcome to **Design & Make It! Textiles Technology for Key Stage 3**. This book will help you succeed in Design and Technology. It tells you all you need to know about working with textiles when designing and making products.

How to use this book

The book starts by explaining about Textiles Technology. The **Project Guide** that follows will be useful throughout your course. It explains the different aspects of doing a Textiles Technology project. These are the skills you will be assessed on.

The book is then divided into six **Units**. Each unit begins by setting you a design challenge. It explains what you need to do to meet the challenge. The pages that follow will:

▷ tell you what you need to know

▷ set tasks for you to do

▷ remind you how to keep a record of what you do.

Unit 1 is about using techniques like embroidery and appliqué to design and make a textile picture.

The focus in **unit 2** is using colour and pattern. You will create a cushion cover with an African style and investigate fabric **properties**.

In **unit 3**, you design patterns for fabrics to furnish an Internet café. You will use computer technologies to help you do this.

Unit 4 is about pattern making and planning. You design and make a bag to sell in a museum gift shop.

The focus in **unit 5** is headwear. Use your knowledge of fabrics to design and make a hat for an adventure holiday company.

Unit 6 is about designing a DIY kit that helps people learn some Indian textile techniques. You will also work in teams to produce a batch of products with an Indian theme.

The final section is the **Textiles Technology Dictionary**. You will find this useful for reference throughout your course. It explains and illustrates the special words and phrases often used in Textiles Technology.

Examples of pupils' design sheets are often provided. These will give you a good idea of the sort of work you need to do.

● On task

These sections will set you tasks to do. Sometimes they will be practical. Sometimes they will ask you to find out more about existing products. Your teacher will tell you which tasks you need to do and when.

On your design sheet

● These boxes will remind you what you need to put on paper as part of your design folder.

● You will be encouraged to use coloured sketches, charts and diagrams as well as words.

Remember

● These boxes will help you revise what you have learned.

● They provide a summary of the key points you need to know.

What is Textiles Technology?

Textiles Technology is one area within the subject called Design and Technology. All areas of Design and Technology involve designing and making things.

Designing and making textile products

The **textiles industry** is one of the world's major industries. We use textiles for all kinds of things, from clothes to curtains and carpets to cushions. There are countless colours, textures and patterns to choose from. There is an extraordinary range of fabrics, each with its own **properties and characteristics**.

Textiles Technology is involved in fabric design, fashion design, theatre and interior design. It's not just about choosing colours, textures and patterns that work well together though. Textile designers also need to consider things like:

▷ how to add colour to fabrics in a variety of ways

▷ how to enrich fabrics with the application of other materials

▷ how different fabric blends and mixtures behave

▷ how textile products can be made economically in large quantities.

To design and make textile products in your Design and Technology lessons you will need to learn more about:

▷ different types of fibres, yarns and fabrics and their properties

▷ joining, cutting, shaping, combining and finishing fabrics

▷ creating, combining and choosing colours, patterns and textures, to achieve a desired effect.

In your lessons you might be asked to design and make things like:

▷ embroidered badges

▷ various fabric bags and containers

▷ T-shirts, waistcoats, hats and other items of clothing

▷ fabrics and soft furnishings (for example, cushions, curtains, lampshades) for specific spaces and places

▷ stage costumes and masks

▷ wall-hangings.

Textiles around the world

Today's textiles are influenced by traditional designs from all over the world. Many are modern versions of ancient textile designs from countries such as South America, India and Africa. Designers are also influenced by other designers and artists. Many of the current methods of constructing and decorating textile products, such as weaving and embroidery, are also very old. However, today's modern technology considerably speeds up the process of manufacture.

Information and Communication Technologies (ICT)

There are plenty of opportunities to use computer-aided design (CAD) when designing textiles products. You may have some pattern design and layout programs available in your school. Perhaps you have some facilities for **computer-aided manufacture** (CAM) too.

Designers use computers a great deal. They help speed up the process of designing and making. They also make it easier to be accurate in your work. You should try to use computers in your design projects.

It's not always appropriate to use a computer, however. Sometimes it's better to **sketch** on paper, or to experiment with some real materials.

Manufacturing

Through this book you'll be introduced to the idea of **manufacturing**. It's one thing to make a single textile product like an embroidered logo in your school workshop. It's quite another to work out how 100, 1000 or 100,000 might be made in a factory.

Working together

Products are rarely designed and made by just one person. It usually involves different teams of people, all working together. As you do the projects in this book, you'll often be invited to share ideas, discuss problems, and take on different roles in making something. You will learn more about how to communicate and co-operate to get a job done on time.

Product analysis

Designers learn a great deal from analysing products that have already been designed and made. They work out what is successful, and what hasn't worked. They then try to make their own designs better.

Try to get into the habit of looking at some of the many textile products that surround you. Think about how well they have been designed and made.

Project Guide

Investigate

In your Design and Technology projects you will need to do some investigation to learn more about:
- the consumers you are designing for
- what they need and want
- what the product might be made from and how it might be made.

To do this you will have to:
- observe and talk to your target consumer group
- consult books, leaflets, booklets, etc.
- contact experts for advice
- use CD-ROMs, software and the Internet.

As you plan and carry out investigation work you need to keep asking yourself whether you are finding out the **right** information. It must be **relevant** to your project.

To **investigate** something means to examine, enquire or find out more about it.

As you design and develop your ideas, make sure you take into account the things you have discovered in your investigation.

Have good ideas

Having good ideas of your own is a very important part of work in Design and Technology.
Experiment with different materials and methods. Think of lots of possible ideas – don't just choose your first idea.

You also need to think about the **design specification** and the **conflicting demands** within it. Look in the Dictionary for more information about these.

As you design, your ideas will change. Make sure you explain why you decided to change them.

Remember that it is very important to record your ideas on your design sheets. Use words and sketches together. Use colour to help explain your ideas.

◎ Develop your design

As you start to finalise your design ideas you need to **test them out**. It would be crazy to make a batch of 100 new jackets if you hadn't tried out the pattern first.

Exactly what do you want to learn from your tests? What do you need to do to get the information you want?

If possible, get people from your target **consumer** group to test your product and say what they think about it.

As always, **presenting your ideas** is very important. You need to be able to show your notes and **sketches** to other people to get their comments and suggestions.

Your work needs to be clear and concise. It needs to show the features of your design: who it's for, its **components** and how it would be made.

◎ Apply what you know (designing)

So what **do** you know already about working with textiles technology? Probably a lot more than you think!

As you work through your projects you will learn a lot about the **properties and characteristics** of the different materials and processes you use. You will get to know what works best and why.

On your design sheets, make it clear how you are applying what you know to your work.

◎ Evaluate

Evaluating products that already exist will help you understand **how** and **why** they have been designed that way.

It's a good idea to **compare** an existing product to other similar products. You should also say what other people say about it. Their views might be different from yours. Include the results of testing.

Use what you have discovered to help you come up with ideas for a new product.

When you evaluate an existing product you need to do more than just describe it. Make sure you also comment on its **quality** – how successful it is. Try to use as many descriptive words as possible.

You also need to evaluate **your own ideas** as you develop your designs. On your design sheet, record things such as:
• which are your best ideas, and why
• how well your ideas might work
• what you plan to do next as a result of evaluating your own work.

Project Guide

◎ Plan the making

Planning what you are doing is a very important aspect of Design and Technology project work. There are so many things to do, you have to work out what **order** to do them in, and **how long** to spend doing them.

Where might **difficulties** occur? What would you do if you ran out of a particular material? At what stages can you check the **quality** of what you are making? Where will you include safety checks?

 COLLECT LOGOS

 COLLECT MATERIALS

DESIGN SHEET

OUTER HAT
↓
Attach logos to front flap.

LINING
↓
Insert labels between two pieces

Make a list of all the things you need to do. Try to sort the list into **main stages** of production – preparing the materials and combining them, and so on. Then put the smaller tasks you need to do in order within each main stage.

Record your planning work on your design sheets. You may need to change your plans when things don't go as expected. Be sure to explain what you did and why.

What needs doing first? What can be done later? How much time do you need to allow for each stage?

◎ Apply what you know (making)

From previous work you have done you should know about things such as:
• the need for safety in workshops
• different production methods.

How can you use what you already know about working with textiles technology?

Try to choose the best materials and tools to make the product you have designed.

Herringbone stitch can be used to trap strips of fabric.

Cross stitch
Chainstitch flower
Couching

DESIGN SHEET

Match what you know about the **characteristics and properties** of materials with the tools and equipment you know you will be able to use.

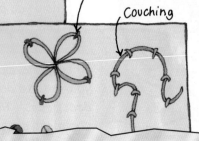

On your design sheets, make it clear how you are applying what you know to your making.

◎ Work with materials

As you make your products, you need to **take care** while you work.

If you are not sure about a particular process, **practise** it first before you make your final product.

Use the tools carefully to join materials together.
Be as **accurate** as you can when you measure.
Organise your tools and your workspace to make your product safely and accurately.

Pay close attention to **safety** precautions while you work.

Carefully explain how you worked on your design sheets. Say what safety precautions you took.

Final evaluation

At the end of your project, think very carefully about how well you have done.

When you tested your final product what did the people it was intended for think?
Maybe they made some useful suggestions for improvements?
How might you change your ideas?
Explain how you tested your final product and what happened.

Finally, how well did **you** work during the project? For example:
• How thorough was your investigation?
• Did you come up with lots of initial ideas, or just one?
• How carefully did you plan the making?
• What were your strengths and weaknesses?

First of all consider the **product** you have designed and made.
• How **successful** is it?
• Does it solve the problem you were given at the start? If not, why not?
• Did it turn out the way you intended? If not, why not?

How could you **improve** the way you work next time? Which aspects of Design and Technology are you going to **target** in your next project? Discuss with your teacher what you will need to do to show you have made **progress**.

Starting Point

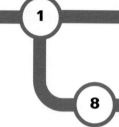

Pictures made from textiles are an interesting way to decorate interior spaces. Can you design and make a textile picture to decorate your school?

Getting the Sack

1

8

Testing and Evaluation

Textiles on display

Your school has an empty display space. The school has asked you to make a textile display for it. You will make a **textile picture** to put on display. As well as looking attractive, your picture must say something about you and your life.

▷ It could be about where you live or the people you live with.

▷ You could do a picture of a family pet. Or your picture could show a special holiday or your favourite possession.

The picture must not be bigger than 20 x 26 cm. It must be framed with card or mounted on a card.

South American textile pictures for sale in a local market.

Textiles on the wall

Textiles are used in people's homes and in the community. They enhance our lives. For centuries, people have used **tapestries** and **wall-hangings** to add warmth and richness to rooms. Tapestries and wall-hangings often tell a story as well.

The famous Bayeux tapestry told the story of King Harold's defeat in 1066.

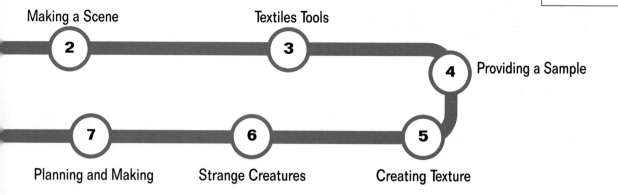

Making a Scene — 2

Textiles Tools — 3

Providing a Sample — 4

Creating Texture — 5

Strange Creatures — 6

Planning and Making — 7

Practice makes perfect

People have been making textile **samplers** for many hundreds of years. People used the first samplers to practise different stitches. However, samplers then became a way of creating a picture. Often the picture showed the family house or garden.

Samplers were very popular in Victorian times.

The focus

In this unit you will have to think carefully about:

▶ the scene you will create for your textile picture

▶ how you will construct the picture using textiles.

The challenge

During this challenge you will use a variety of textiles techniques. For example:

▶ machine-stitching

▶ stitching by hand – embroidery

▶ appliqué – collage

You may already be familiar with some of these techniques. You will have the opportunity to learn them all, and decide which ones are best for your textile picture.

The end product

You will produce a textile picture to display in your school. The picture will show something special to you.

It will be mounted for display in a frame.

Getting the Sack

Study other designs that are similar to what you intend to design and make.

This will help you understand how to design and make your own textile products.

'Arpillera' means sacking. People used old grain sacks to support the picture.

The picture is made of scraps of fabrics sewn onto a background. This is called **appliqué**. Here a mixture of new and recycled fabrics are stitched to the sacking.

Each scene is created from vividly coloured cloth. It is set against the backdrop of the Andes mountains.

The pictures are beautifully stitched and show a high standard of skill.

South American Arpilleras

South America has a very rich craft work tradition. Local markets display weaving, embroidery, baskets, ceramics and musical instruments.

Women started to make **Arpilleras** in Chile in the 1970s. These pictures were a protest against poverty and injustice. They were sold to make much needed money for the family.

Today people make designs for the tourists. They sell them through charities to countries in the West. The pictures show scenes of village life in the Andes mountains.

South America

Chile

Tiny three-dimensional dolls show everyday activities. The dolls are carefully dressed, with hair and embroidered features.

There are figures made from wire, bound with thread. Each one is clothed in tiny detail. They may be playing musical instruments or carrying tools. Some figures may be returning from market with a tiny basket of shopping.

There is a pocket in the back of the Arpillera. Neatly folded in the pocket is a letter telling the story shown on the front.

The picture is finished around the border with a blanket stitch.

● On task Investigate

1. Look in books or use other sources to find examples of appliqué or tapestry work. **Sketch** and make notes about what you find, on design sheet **1**. Say how you think the pictures have been made. Use the example on this page as a guide.

2. What can you discover about the Bayeux tapestry? What story does it tell? Add your answer to design sheet **1**.

I looked at home and in shops for examples of how appliqué is used today. I found:

CLOTHES   OVEN GLOVES   DESIGN SHEET 1   TOWEL   CUSHION   BAGS

On your design sheet

- Record your investigation into other examples of appliqué or tapestry work. **1**
- Write down what you find out about the Bayeux tapestry. **1**

Remember

- Investigating existing products is a very good starting point for designers.

Making a Scene

Can you create a scene as colourful and interesting as an Arpillera?

Spider diagram centred on **Textile Picture** with branches:
- Dancing lessons
- On holiday
- Me and my pet
- Going out with friends
- Day-trip to the seaside
- My favourite hobby – painting playing, football
- Eating my favourite meal – pizza and ice cream
- My favourite film

● On task 1
Have good ideas

1. Create a spider diagram that records some good subjects for your picture. Try not to reject any ideas at this stage. Draw your spider diagram at the top of design sheet **2a**.

2. Discuss your diagram with a partner. Add any more ideas you have.

Design specification

It is useful to write a **design specification** before you start designing. This is a list that states clearly what features your design must have.

● On task 2 Investigate

At the bottom of design sheet **2a** write a design specification for your textile picture. Answer the following questions as full sentences.

▶ What size will it be?

▶ What must be in my textile picture?

▶ What is my picture for?

▶ Who is going to see it?

▶ How is it going to be displayed?

DESIGN SPECIFICATION

Our new range of socks must be:
- warm and cosy for the weaver
- attractive to look at
- made from a durable. hard-wearing material
- a knitted fabric to ensure a snug fit
- easy to care for, i.e. must wash well and not shrink

First thoughts

It is always useful to think of several ideas at this stage. Your first idea is not always the best one.

Sometimes combining parts of different ideas can create unexpectedly pleasing results.

● *On task 3 Develop your design*

1. On design sheet **2b** make quick **sketches** of your ideas for an interesting scene. Make sure you have at least six different ideas. Base your sketches on your spider diagram. Don't worry about detail at this stage. Use notes and colour to help explain your ideas. Try combining some ideas together and see what happens.

2. Discuss your ideas with your partner and ask others in your group. This is often helpful, as talking to others can help you develop your ideas.

On your design sheets

● Draw a spider diagram of subjects for your textile picture. **2a**

● Write a design specification for your picture. **2a**

● Make quick sketches of your ideas and discuss them with others. **2b**

Remember

● It is useful to write a specification before designing. This reminds you of everything to be included in your design.

Textiles Tools

3

Before starting practical work you need to know what tools and equipment you can use. You must also know how to use them safely and how to look after them.

Measuring

Accurate measuring helps make sure everything is the correct size.

Rulers

A transparent ruler is best.

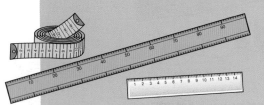

Metre sticks

Useful for measuring longer lengths.

Tape measures

About 150 cm long. They can measure round curved shapes, because they are flexible.

Marking out

You sometimes need to put marks on the fabric as a guide to help you cut out. There are different ways to do this.

Tailors' chalk

This comes in different colours, and is traditionally used by tailors. It can be removed easily from the fabric afterwards.

Water-soluble pens

You can easily remove marks made by water-soluble pens, using a damp cloth.

Pencils

Sometimes a light pencil is fine, but do not use biro or felt pens.

Cutting out

Cutting shears

The blades must be 15–20 cm long to give a long smooth cutting motion. Cutting shears must only be used for fabrics. Cutting paper with them will make them blunt.

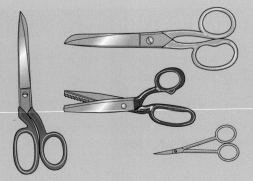

All-purpose scissors

Good for cutting out paper patterns, light cutting and thread trimming.

Embroidery scissors

These are small and sharp. Good for trimming threads.

Joining

After cutting out, the next stage is usually to join pieces of fabric together.

Glues

Use glues sparingly or they seep through the fabric. They smell quite strong, so if possible use them near an open window.

Needles

To join fabric by sewing you will need a needle. These come in different sizes with different sized eyes. You need to pick the right one for your fabric and yarn.

Sharps are medium sized needles that are good for general-purpose sewing.

Embroidery/Crewel needles have long eyes to take one or more threads of stranded cotton.

Tapestry needles have blunt points, which slip between fabric yarns without splitting them. They can be used with wool or thick embroidery cotton on open mesh fabric such as hessian.

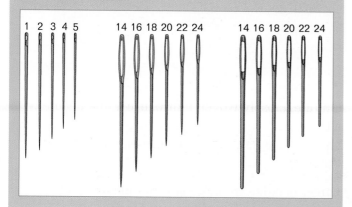

When something goes wrong

A seam ripper is handy for slitting machine stitches when unpicking. Be careful not to slit the material.

General safety points for the workroom

▷ Don't run.

▷ Do not distract others when they are working.

▷ Put everything away in the right place when you have finished.

▷ Never put needles or pins in your mouth. Keep them in a needle case or pin cushion.

▷ All scissors are sharp and can be dangerous.

When carrying scissors always hold them by the blades to avoid accidents.

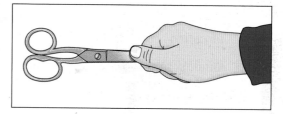

● *On task Apply what you know*

Design a safety poster on design sheet **3**. It should illustrate the most important safety points to remember when working in a textiles workshop.

On your design sheet

● Design a textiles workshop safety poster. **3**

Remember

● Tools and equipment need to be looked after properly.

● Scissors must always be carried by the blades.

● Pins and needles should be kept in a pin cushion or needle case.

Providing a Sample

In the Picture

It is a good idea to make a sampler to practise your stitching on. This will also help you learn about tools and equipment.

A sampler

A **sampler** is a small piece of fabric on which you can try out different stitches and ideas (see page 13). This allows you to experiment before working on your final picture. This helps avoid problems later on.

For your sampler you will need:

▷ yarns and threads, of various thicknesses

▷ background fabric to work on, such as hessian or calico

▷ small scraps of fabric for further experimentation.

Using an embroidery frame

Handling fabric and keeping it flat while you sew can be tricky. An **embroidery frame** can help overcome this problem.

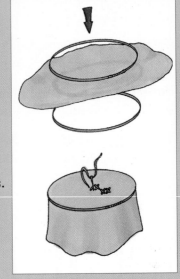

1 Place your fabric over the first hoop.

2 Place the second hoop over the fabric.

3 Make sure the fabric is taut between the hoops. Tighten the screw to keep the fabric in position.

On fine, closely woven fabric, use a fine needle with a fine yarn. You will struggle to get a large blunt tapestry needle through it. You might also damage the fabric.

Larger needles are more appropriate for thicker yarns and more loosely woven fabrics.

During this project you may need to use different needles and yarns on the different fabrics you choose for your picture.

In stitches

A stitch is a length of thread passed through, and back through, a piece of fabric. It can be used to sew one piece of fabric to another. Stitches can also make decorative patterns.

1 Thread needle. Tie a knot in the end of the thread.

2 Bring the needle up through the fabric where you want the stitch to start.

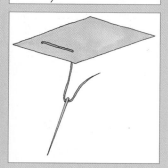

3 Bring it back down where you want the stitch to end.

4 Finish off by bringing the needle through to the back of your work. Make several small stitches on this one spot before cutting the thread.

● On task 1 Work with materials

Make a sampler of your own.

1. Add stitches to make your own patterns.

2. Try out different yarns.

3. Try out different colours.

● On task 2 Apply what you know

Note down any new tools and equipment you have learned about, on design sheet **4**.

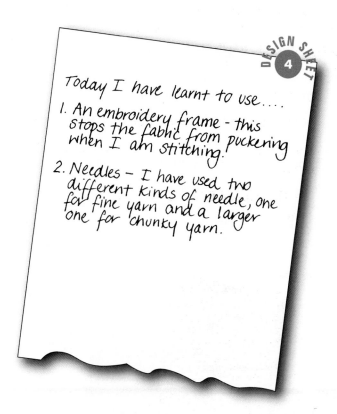

DESIGN SHEET 4

Today I have learnt to use....

1. An embroidery frame - this stops the fabric from puckering when I am stitching.

2. Needles - I have used two different kinds of needle, one for fine yarn and a larger one for chunky yarn.

On your design sheet

● Note down what tools and equipment you learned about. **4**

Remember

● Testing out stitches and techniques helps to ensure that the final product will be of a high quality.

Creating Texture

In the Picture

There are ways to add more texture and depth to your work. Experiment with one or two of the following techniques.

Panamanian Cuna Indian textile.

Appliqué

Appliqué means 'to apply'. You can apply pieces of fabric to a background and stitch them into position.

● On task 1 Work with materials

1. Cut out some shapes from scrap materials and arrange them on your sampler.

2. Try arranging the shapes in different ways to make patterns.

3. Experiment by overlapping the shapes.

4. Investigate ways of holding your fabric in position while you stitch it (see page 60). Choose one way, and then use a variety of stitches to sew the shapes to the background.

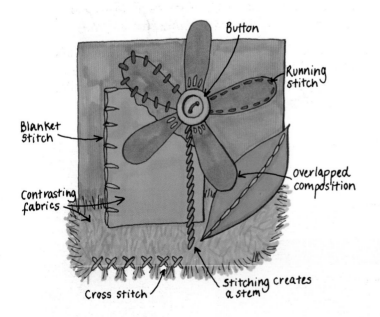

Padding

You can stuff sections of your appliqué to make them stand out even more.

Stuffing

Remember
The stitching should not be too big or too far apart. If it is, the stuffing will come out.

● On task 2 Work with materials

1. Sew around most of the shape you want to pad, but leave a small gap at the end.

2. Push some stuffing into the small gap.

3. Sew up the gap. Remember to finish off on the back of your work.

4. Alternatively, you can stitch down the entire shape. Then cut a small hole in the back, stuff, and sew up the hole.

Couching

Hand-stitching can be very time-consuming. If you have a large area to fill in, or you want to create lines, you could try **couching**.

Couching is a traditional embroidery stitch. You lay down yarn onto fabric in a pattern and stitch it into place. If you experiment you can create some dramatic effects.

Elizabethans often used couching to decorate their clothing.

1 Lie the whole length of yarn on top of the fabric in the pattern you want.

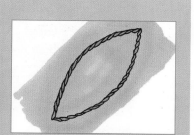

2 Pin the yarn at intervals in about the right position.

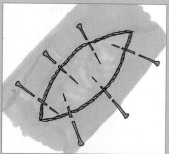

3 Couch down the yarn at intervals using a straight up and down, or 'stab', stitch.

4 You could use a contrasting colour to couch it down.

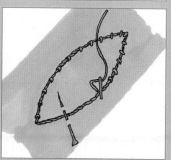

● *On task 4 Evaluate*

1. On design sheet **5**, write a brief account of the experiments you have done to add texture and depth to your work. Say which techniques you think have been the most successful, and why.

2. Look back to your initial ideas on design sheet **2b**. Choose four of your design ideas. On the bottom of design sheet **5** suggest appropriate techniques for each design.

● *On task 3 Work with new materials*

Experiment with couching on your sampler.

On your design sheet

● Record the techniques you have tried. **5**

● Suggest the best techniques for your design ideas. **5**

Remember

● To create texture you can use couching, appliqué and padding.

● Use a combination of techniques to get the right effect.

Strange Creatures

You could include a figure in your picture, or perhaps some strange creature. Here are some ideas. Which technique will get you the result you want?

Manipulating fabrics

Tying, bunching, wrapping and knotting can be used to produce figures or creatures. You can stitch the figures onto your wall-hanging.

Loose fabric is tied to create a structure or form.

Mexican textile dolls.

Elastic fabrics

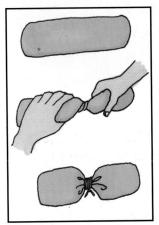

Old socks and tights are excellent for making figures. You can stuff, twist, manipulate and tie them into realistic or fantasy shapes.

Fabric is wrapped around the pipe cleaner limbs to make a more realistic body shape.

Wool or string 'hair'?

Cross stitch 'buttons'.

Simple cotton dress.

Wool is wrapped around pipe cleaner to make shoes.

Pipe cleaner body.

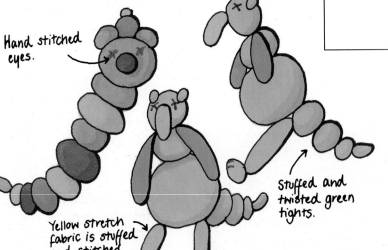

Hand stitched eyes.

Stuffed and twisted green tights.

Yellow stretch fabric is stuffed and stitched to the body.

Designing people

Start with a skeleton. Pipe cleaners are useful for making skeletons. You can cut and bend them into many shapes and sizes.

You can then wrap your skeletons in fabrics to create clothing. You can add details using stitching.

Design development

Trying out different techniques makes it easier to imagine what your wall-hanging might look like. Remember to look at your **design specification** to remind yourself what is required for your textile picture. This will help you develop your design successfully.

● On task 1 Evaluate

Look carefully at the ideas you sketched on design sheet **2b**. Consider what you have learned from making a sampler. Choose one picture that you think will look eye-catching when displayed.

Write down which picture you have chosen at the top of design sheet **6**. Explain why you have chosen this one.

Hanging it up

There are several ways to hang your wall-hanging. Discuss in groups the most effective way to display your work.

Unusual shapes may look better mounted on card. Here the card mount has been painted to look like a plate.

A card frame can be given an interesting texture when wrapped in strips of fabric and yarn.

● On task 2 Develop your design

1. **Sketch** your final design in more detail on design sheet **6**. Add colour. You may decide to simplify your design to make it easier to make.

2. Mark in the stitching. What will the stitches look like and where will they go? Label the techniques you will use.

On your design sheet

- Choose your final design. Explain why you have chosen this one. **6**

- Sketch and colour in a detailed version of your final design. **6**

- Explain how you will make your wall-hanging. **6**

Remember

- Look at all your ideas carefully before finalising your design. You can combine ideas to create the best possible solution.

25

Planning and Making

Careful preparation will help you create a well-made textile picture.

Creating a background

You will need a background fabric. You can sew all the different pieces of your picture onto this background. Make newspaper templates the exact sizes and shapes of the different pieces to help you cut them out accurately.

The background fabric should be a medium-weight, firm fabric. If it is too thin or stretchy, it will not support the fabrics for your design. Your teacher will probably have something suitable.

Creating symmetry

You may wish to include shapes in your wall-hanging that are **symmetrical**. This means that they are the same size and shape on each side.

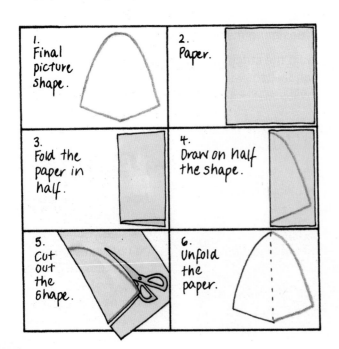

Cutting out

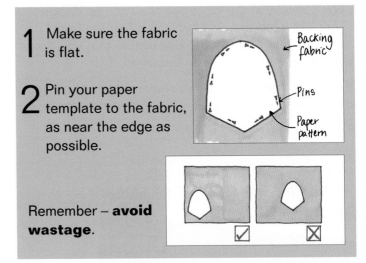

1 Make sure the fabric is flat.

2 Pin your paper template to the fabric, as near the edge as possible.

Remember – **avoid wastage**.

Finding fabrics

Look carefully through all the fabric scraps available to you. Select the right colours, textures and weights to get the effects you want.

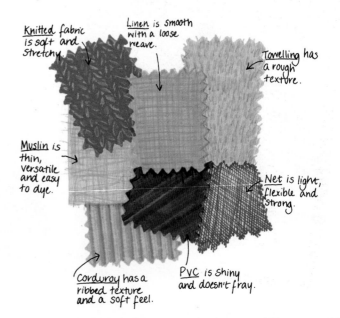

Planning matters

Prepare to be flexible! Everything may not go according to plan. You may have to change things as you go along. Something you planned may be too difficult or time-consuming. You may think of a better way to do things.

● On task 1 Plan the making

You should now know everything you need to do to create your wall-hanging. On design sheet **7**, write out a simple plan for the order in which you will make the wall-hanging.

DESIGN SHEET 7

• Order of Making
1. Cut out background panels and appliqué shapes.
2. Machine stitch together the background sky and sand panels.
3. Use scissors to cut fringing into the dog's head and body panels. Handstitch panels to the background.
4. Use decorative stitches to apply starfish to the sand.
5. Use a strong thread to stitch stones to the sand.
6. Glue on dog collar, nose and eyes.
7. Finally hand sew on name tag and buttons for eyes.

Creating the picture

● On task 2 Work with material

Cut out the pieces for your wall-hanging. Start to arrange the pieces on the background fabric. Put the biggest pieces on the background first and then build up the smaller pieces on top.

You might be able to sew through several layers at the same time. Your teacher will advise you on this.

Using the sewing machine

If you have access to a sewing machine, you could use it to sew on the larger parts of your design. Smaller pieces and details can be hand-stitched.

On your design sheet

● Plan the order of making. **7**

Remember

● Careful planning will lead to quality products.

● You may need to alter plans and ideas as you work through a project.

Testing and Evaluation

When your wall-hanging is finished, find out how successful it is. Here are some ways you could test your wall-hanging.

Testing times

Finding out what other people think about your work is always useful. Work together in groups of three or four.

● On task 1 Final evaluation

Each person in the group should present their work to the others. You could describe to the group:

▶ why you chose your idea

▶ the things you are pleased with

▶ how you coped with any problems during making

▶ any changes you made.

The rest of the group could then feed back their thoughts and ideas about your project to you.

Write down what happened and what people said about your work, on design sheet **8a**.

A wider audience

Perhaps you could invite other people to see your wall-hangings if they are all displayed together somewhere accessible.

● On task 2 Final evaluation

Find out other people's thoughts and feelings about the display. You could do this by:

▶ giving each visitor a short questionnaire to fill in

▶ providing a Visitors' Book in which people can write comments.

Add your findings to design sheet **8a**.

● On task 3 Final evaluation

Read each point on your **design specification**, on design sheet **2a**. Consider carefully whether you have achieved everything you intended. Write your findings in your final evaluation, on design sheet **8b**.

● On task 4 Final evaluation

When you write your final evaluation on design sheet **8b**, comment about the following things:

► what you thought about it

► what other people thought about it

► the design (Is it eye-catching, bright and lively?)

► the making (Is it well made? Is there a good variety of stitches and techniques? How could it be improved?)

Finally, pick a wall-hanging from the display made by someone else. Explain why you particularly like it.

On your design sheets

- Write down comments from your group presentation or exhibition. **8a**

- Record your final evaluation. **8b**

Remember

- It is important to give positive criticism about other people's work and your own.

- You need to give reasons why you do or do not like something about your work.

Starting Point

People like their homes to look stylish, warm and welcoming. They use textile products to help achieve the effect they want.

Can you design and make a cushion cover that reflects an African theme?

Adinkra

1

10

An Interview with...
Lesley Johnson

As well as using textiles to make clothes, we use them to enhance our surroundings and make our lives more 'comfortable'.

We do this by using 'soft furnishings' in our homes, such as cushions and curtains.

Can you design some attractive and fashionable cushion covers?

Read the letter on the right. It is from a company that specialises in African artefacts.

Dear Designer,

My shops specialise in products that reflect an African theme. I am hoping to add some soft furnishings and textiles to my product range. I believe there is a big market for these.

My customers are mostly in the 18–35 age group. They are interested in current fashion trends that reflect ethnic designs.

I have recently received some Adinkra cloth from Ghana, which I will be selling. I would like a range of cushion covers to co-ordinate with this cloth. These should be about 32 x 32 cm. Each cushion cover should have an Adinkra symbol as the main design. I have enclosed some photographs of this cloth to help you with your designs.

I look forward to seeing your first ideas.

Yours sincerely,

Adinkra cloth from Ghana. Adrinkra cloth is printed using special blocks, shown on the right (see also page 33).

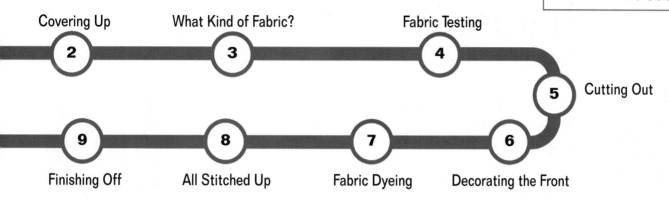

Covering Up — 2

What Kind of Fabric? — 3

Fabric Testing — 4

5 — Cutting Out

9 — Finishing Off

8 — All Stitched Up

7 — Fabric Dyeing

6 — Decorating the Front

The challenge

Can you design and make a cushion cover for this company? To meet this challenge you must think carefully about how cushion covers are constructed. This will involve evaluating existing products.

The focus

In this unit you will focus on making something three-dimensional in textiles. You will also consider different ways of applying your African design to the cushion cover.

The end product

You will design and make a cushion cover. To be successful it must:

▶ be similar in style to the Adinkra fabrics

▶ measure 32 x 32 cm

▶ be easy to take on and off the cushion

▶ be of a good quality so that people will want to buy it.

Button fastening.

Popper fastening.

Tie fastenings.

Tassel fastening.

How can cushion covers be fastened together?

Andinkra stamps.

Adinkra

1

What is Adinkra cloth and how is it made? How will you apply your design to fabric? These are some of the things you will need to find out in your investigation.

The Adinkra cloth of Ghana

Africa has a very strong textiles tradition. For centuries Africans have used weaving, dyeing and printing. They often use bold colours and patterns.

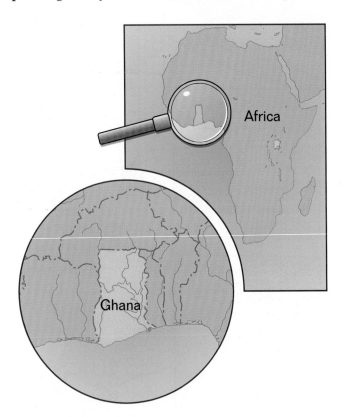

It is believed that the art of **Adinkra** came from a village called Gyaman where chief Adinkra ruled. The word Adinkra means 'farewell' or 'goodbye'. This special cloth was used for funerals to say goodbye to the departed.

The foundation of the Adinkra cloth is a plain white cotton, or cotton dyed russet brown.

Symbols

A **symbol** is a sign, shape or object that represents a person, idea or value.

The people of Ghana use simple shapes to decorate Adinkra fabrics. They give each shape a meaning. The shape symbolises the meaning.

There are over fifty symbols for Adinkra cloth. The ones shown here represent the heart, the house, and unity.

● On task 1 Investigate

Look in books and on the Internet to find out more about weaving and dyeing in traditional African textiles. You could carry out this investigation in pairs and present your findings to the rest of the group. Record what you discover on design sheet **1a**.

What dyes do they use?

The dye used for block printing is made from the bark of a tree (called Ashanti 'Badie'). The bark is cut up and boiled with several lumps of iron. This is boiled for several hours and then the water is strained off. This dark brown liquid is the Adinkra stamping dye.

Printing blocks

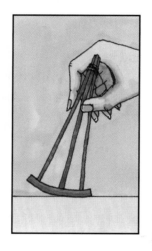

The Adinkra cloth is block printed. The printing blocks are made from calabashes. A calabash is a bit like a large pumpkin that grows underground. When it dries out it leaves a hard shell from which printing blocks can be cut. The blocks have small sticks leading from the stamp to a point. This means that they can be held between the thumb and forefinger.

DESIGN SHEET 1b

My own symbol for "community"

"Sanctity"

I like this symbol, it may look better with a border.

Examples of borders. This one may be too complicated.

This symbol will make a good repeat.

● On task 2 Have good ideas

On design sheet **1b**, design some symbols of your own in a style similar to the Adinkra symbols. Give each symbol a meaning.

On your design sheets

- Describe weaving and dyeing in African textile traditions. **1a**

- Design some symbols in a similar style to the Adinkra symbols. Explain what each of your symbols means. **1b**

Remember

- A symbol is a sign, shape or object that represents a person, idea or value.

Covering Up

Look at some existing cushion covers. Then you can start to design your own cover.

Button fastening up the centre back.

Painted gold star with green top stitch.

Cotton inner cushion.

stuffing

Care label concealed inside the cover in the seam of the inner cushion.

DESIGN SHEET **2a**

Product analysis

To help you understand cushion covers, it is a good idea to examine some existing products. This is called product **analysis**.

▷ How are they **designed**?

▷ How are they **made**?

▷ What kinds of stitching are used?

Inside the seam allowance has been ironed open and stitched down.

This top stitch gives a good finish on both sides of the cushion and is an interesting detail when done in a contrasting colour.

DESIGN SHEET **2a**

● On task 1 Evaluate

Bring some cushion covers from home if possible. In groups discuss the following:

► How is the decoration applied to the cover?

► What sort of fastening is used?

► Where is the stitching? (Turn the cover inside out.)

► How big is the seam allowance?

► Are the edges finished?

► Which jobs were done first and which last?

► How well designed and made do you think each cover is?

Choose one of the covers. Record your own study of it on design sheet **2a**.

Design specification

You have studied how cushion covers are designed and made. So now you can add some more detail to the brief the shop owner gave you (see page 30). This will become your **design specification** – a checklist of things your design must do to be successful. Write this at the top of design sheet **2b**.

> ### DESIGN SPECIFICATION FOR CUSHION COVER
>
> 1. My cushion cover must co-ordinate with the Adinkra fabric by using similar colours and shapes.
>
> 2. The cover must fit a cushion of 32 x 32 cm.
>
> 3. It must be easy to take on and off the cushion pad so that it can be washed.
>
> 4. The design and making must be of good quality to attract buyers.

● On task 2 Develop your design

Sketch some designs for the front and back of your cushion cover.
You need to think about:

► where the Adinkra design motif will go

► fastenings, such as zips, buttons, and so on.

Remember to add labels to your sketches. Work on design sheet **2b**.

● On task 3 Develop your design

Finalise your design. **Sketch** the front and back of your final design on design sheet **2c**. Explain why you have decided on the method of fastening you have chosen.

DESIGN SHEET 2b

Button fastening is secure but how do I make the button holes?

I could sew on loops of cord instead

This design could be improved by painting a frame around the symbol.

Cushion pad slides in here.

Block print design

A tie fastening in a contrasting colour will add interest to my design.

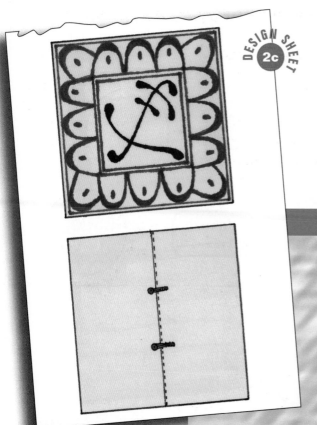

DESIGN SHEET 2c

On your design sheets

● Present your analysis of a cushion. **2a**

● Write your design specification. **2b**

● Draw and label some sketches of your cushion cover. **2b**

● Sketch the front and back of your final design. **2c**

Remember

● It is important to be aware of the needs of potential users so that they will be interested in buying your product.

● Product analysis is a useful tool for examining existing products.

● Use what you learn from carrying out a product analysis to help you with your designing.

What Kind of Fabric?

Out of Africa
Out of Africa

The fabric you choose is important. Some fabrics are woven and some are knitted. The way the fabric is made gives it a particular look and feel.

Cotton calico would be an ideal fabric for your cushion cover. It is a medium-weight plain weave that is easy to work with. It also absorbs fabric paint and dye well. The slight rough texture will give your cushion cover an authentic African feel.

Cottoning on

Cotton is made from **natural** fibres. Cotton fibres come from the cotton plant. Up until the twentieth century only natural fibres were available. **Synthetic** fibres were invented in the early twentieth century.

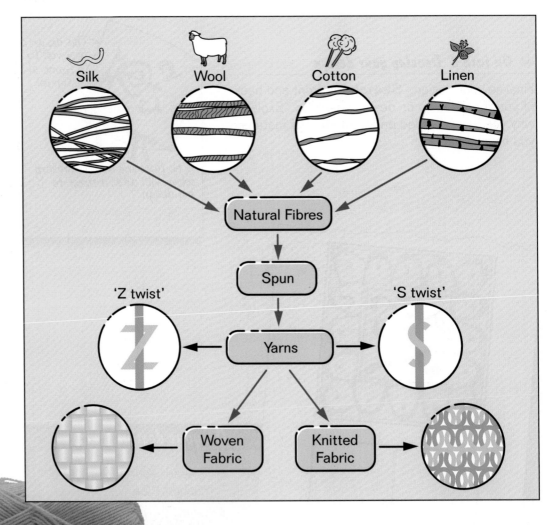

Silk Wool Cotton Linen

Natural Fibres

Spun

'Z twist' Yarns 'S twist'

Woven Fabric Knitted Fabric

DESIGN SHEET 3a

Sample A - Herringbone weave.
Most effective when woven in
contrasting colours which
accentuate the zig-zag pattern.
When woven in heavy wool is
used for suiting and tailoring.

Sample B - Satin weave.
Very smooth and shiny.
Smooth yarn is woven tightly
to produce a fabric suitable
for night wear and luxury
products.

Sample C - Plain weave.
A simple weave that lends
itself to natural and hairy
yarns. Softer fabrics such as
linen, sacking and poplin
use this weave.

● On task 1 Investigate

1. Your teacher will give you some samples of woven fabrics. Examine them under a magnifying lens. Record what you discover on design sheet **3a**.

2. Pull out the yarns from some woven fabrics. Stick the fabric swatches on design sheet **3a** along with yarns you have pulled out. Describe each of the types of yarn or fabric by answering the following questions:

   ▶ Is the yarn or fabric smooth, rough, hairy, bobbly, fine or thick?

   ▶ How is the fabric woven? Is it a simple plain weave?

   ▶ Are the yarns twisted tightly or loosely?

   ▶ What products might each fabric be suitable for?

● On task 2 Investigate / Apply what you know

1. Find some knitted fabrics. On design sheet **3b** answer these questions:

   ▶ How are the fabrics constructed? Do they have a warp and weft?

   ▶ How are they different from your woven samples?

   ▶ What sorts of products are knitted fabrics used for?

2. At home, find examples of knitted and woven fabrics. What are they used for and why?

• Looking through a lens at knitted samples

DESIGN SHEET 3b

SAMPLE Ⓐ

Front:
Smooth feel
because the
knit is so
tight and
small.

Back:
This fabric
is soft and
of medium weight.
Suitable for making
'T'shirts or pyjamas.

SAMPLE Ⓑ

Back:
This sample is thicker and
fluffy on the back. It would
be suitable for making garments
that are meant to keep the
wearer warm e.g. sweatshirt.

On your design sheets

● Take some woven fabrics apart. Describe each of them. **3a**

● Describe some knitted fabrics you have studied. **3b**

Remember

● There are many different fabrics, each with different properties.

● Fabrics can be constructed by either weaving or knitting yarns.

● Fabrics are woven or knitted depending on the intended end-use.

Fabric Testing

There are many tests you can carry out on your fabric. Testing will ensure that the fabric has the right properties for a cushion cover.

Durability

Checking it out

In industry, the fabrics used to make textile products are always thoroughly tested before they are used. This is to make sure that they have the right properties for the planned product. Testing also makes sure the fabric is of the right quality, with no faults.

Stiffness

Properties

Different fabrics have different **properties**, which allows for a variety of end-uses.

Finishes

Different finishes can be applied to fabric after it has been made. These finishes improve the quality and properties of the fabric.

Softness

Easy-care

Soil resistance

Flame retardance

Stain resistance

● *On task 1 Apply what you know*

1. In groups, discuss which properties and finishes are the most important for your design.

2. Write a specification for your ideal fabric on design sheet **4a**.

Testing for absorbency

Your fabric may need to be dyed. This process is explained on page 42. It is very important that the fabric you use will absorb the fabric paint well, or the dye if you are using batik.

● On task 2 Investigate

In groups, carry out a test for absorbency. You could:

▶ compare a natural fabric with a synthetic fabric (for example, cotton and polyester)

▶ find out how much moisture the fibres of the fabric can absorb.

Write down how you did your tests, and record the results, on design sheet **4b**.

Absorbency

Flammability

1 Use scales to find the mass of each fabric sample.

2 Immerse the samples in water.

3 Find the new mass of each sample. Work out the absorbency of each sample, like this:

$$absorbency = \frac{increase\ mass\ \times 100\%}{original\ mass}$$

4 Alternatively, try dipping each sample in dye for the same amount of time. Observe what happens. Some fabrics produce a stronger colour than others.

5 Record the results and conclusions of your tests on design sheet **4b**. Mount your samples to illustrate your results.

DESIGN SHEET 4a

- Fabric specification for cushion cover
- Should be soft to provide comfort for the user.
- Needs to be made from an absorbent fabric so it can absorb dyes.
- Medium weight - not too stiff.
- Durable - so that it wears well.
- Easy to wash, dry and iron. A stain/soil resistant finish would help.
- Flame retardant finish would make it safer for use in the home.

On your design sheets

- Write your ideal fabric specification. **4a**
- Test your fabrics and record the results. **4b**

Remember

- Choosing the right fabric is vital for producing quality products.

Cutting Out

Before you can decorate the front of your cushion cover, you need to cut out the fabric. It is necessary to make a flat pattern before cutting out.

Making a pattern

In textiles a flat **pattern** is a paper template. Making a template to cut round ensures that you will cut your fabric to the right size. This prevents wastage.

● On task 1 Develop your design

Make a paper pattern that you can use to cut out your fabric. Use the instructions on this page. Make sure you understand how the back and front pieces go together.

1 On a piece of paper, draw the front of your cushion using the correct measurements. Use a ruler.

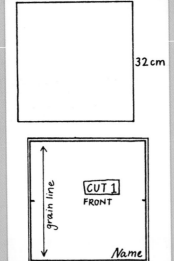

32 cm

32 cm

grain line

CUT 1
FRONT

Name

2 Add 1 cm all the way around. This is called a **seam allowance**. Add the pattern markings as shown in the diagram.

3 The pattern piece for the back needs to be half the size of the front.
$$\frac{32}{2} \text{ cm} = 16 \text{ cm}$$

32 cm

16 cm

centre back

4 Add 5 cm to the centre back to provide an overlap. Add a seam allowance.

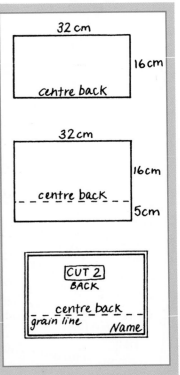

32 cm

16 cm

centre back

5 cm

CUT 2
BACK

centre back

grain line

Name

Cutting out waste

● On task 2 Investigate

In a group, examine a small piece of fabric. Discuss:

► what the warp, weft and bias are

► what a grain line is for.

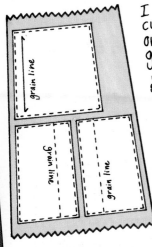

I will cut my cushion pieces out on the straight grain. This will give my cushion strength and stability.

I will add extra fabric to each seam. This will allow me to sew my pattern pieces together and still create a cushion the size I originally intended.

DESIGN SHEET **5**

● On task 3 Apply what you know

Illustrate the cutting out process on design sheet **5**, applied to your design. Add notes to explain why the seam allowance and grain line are important.

On your design sheet

● Illustrate the cutting out process needed for your design. **5**

Remember

● A seam allowance is necessary to ensure that your final product is not too small.

● Avoid wastage when cutting out materials.

Decorating the Front

There are many ways to apply your symbol or design to the front of your cushion cover. Some ways involve simple drawing or painting. Other techniques are much more complex. Which one will you use?

There are many ways you could apply your symbol to the front:

▷ fabric paints

▷ fabric pens and crayons

▷ block printing.

▷ batik.

Some techniques will give you a positive image, others a negative image. Whichever technique you choose, it is important to prepare the fabric properly.

● **On task   Investigate**

1. Investigate some of the methods shown on this page for applying your design. Your teacher may suggest some other possibilities. Record what you discover on design sheet **6a**.

2. Try out some pens, paints and crayons on scrap fabric. Describe the different effects they give on design sheet **6b**.

Preparing the fabric for painting or dyeing

1 Wash your fabric to remove any impurities or finishes that might prevent the colour being absorbed.

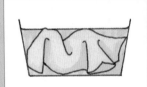

2 Iron your fabric to get rid of any creases.

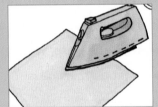

3 Fix your fabric to a flat surface with either masking tape or drawing pins.

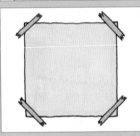

4 Mark out your design onto the fabric using chalk, water-soluble pen or very light pencil.

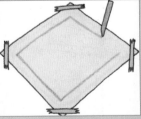

5 For batik you could use a dark marker to draw your design on paper. Place the paper under the fabric so the design shows through.

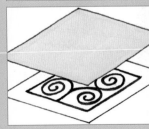

Fabric painting

1 Use a brush to paint on your design. Do not use water with the fabric paint as it will run.

2 Allow the paint to dry.

3 Iron your fabric. This will fix the colour into your fabric and prevent the colour running when washed.

• PAINTS
- Very flexible and can cover large areas.
- Not always easy to control.
- Can be layered or mixed to create another colour.

• CRAYONS
- When used on their side they can create interesting textures.
- They can be used to make thick, chunky lines and on top of other mediums like paint.

• PENS
- Excellent for fine lines and adding detail to painted areas.

DESIGN SHEET 6b

Batik

Batik is a **resist** technique. Where wax is applied the fabric will remain its original colour.

1 Use a brush or traditional Tjanting to apply the wax on your design. A brush is easier! It is important to ensure that the wax goes right through the fabric.

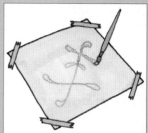

2 Let the wax go hard and cool. Then leave your fabric in the dye. Rinse your fabric and leave it to dry.

3 Next remove the wax. Place your work between two pieces of newspaper and apply a hot iron. Repeat until no more wax is absorbed into the newspaper.

4 Finally, remove any wax residue by washing in warm soapy water.

On your design sheets

• Investigate different methods of adding your design to the cushion cover. **6a**

• Describe the different effects you get when using pens, paints and crayons. **6b**

Remember

• It is important to iron any fabric you paint in order to fix the colour.

Fabric Dyeing

Out of Africa

Dyes are used to change the colour of textiles. Dyes can be made from natural or chemical sources.

Making colour

There are many dyes and fabric paints available to buy in the shops.

In Africa, many people still use dyes that they have mixed themselves from natural sources. The Adinkra dye was made from tree bark.

Dyeing

Dyeing involves all the material being completely immersed in dye solution. This can be done at one of four stages in the production process:

1. fibre
2. yarn
3. fabric
4. completed garment or product.

Dyeing is different from printing. In **printing**, colour is applied just to the surface of the fabric.

Industrial testing of textile dyes.

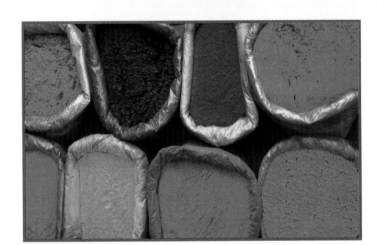

Dyeing and the environment

Textile dyeing processes can have a large **environmental impact**. They uses vast amounts of water, and dyes and other chemicals get transferred to the effluent (waste water). The polluted water is unsightly, often toxic and not quickly biodegradable. New processes are now being developed that do not pollute the effluent, and which use far less water.

Natural dyes

Natural dyes such as those used by the Andinkra are made from a variety of sources such as plants and vegetables. They are very time-consuming to make and so are rarely used today. Some artists and crafts people like to make natural dyes as they can create very subtle colour effects. Natural dyes have quite unpredictable outcomes, which can also be appealing in art and craft work.

Synthetic dyes

Synthetic, chemical dyes were developed in the 1850s. By the beginning of the twentieth century synthetic dyes were used for most of the coloured textiles produced in Europe and North America. Synthetic dyes have a number of advantages. Synthetic dyes are:

▷ available in a wider range of colours

▷ brighter

▷ much cheaper

▷ each made to a scientific formula so the same colour can be reproduced repeatedly.

There are also many disadvantages with using natural dyes:

▷ it is harder to predict the final outcome of a natural dye

▷ it is extremely difficult to mix the exact same colour again and again

▷ growing enough of the appropriate plants would use up very large amounts of land.

Programming a computer-controlled dyeing vat.

Fabric dyeing in Latvia.

- WEARING AN APRON AND RUBBER GLOVES PROTECTS YOU FROM ANY DYE SPLASHES.

- ALWAYS HANDLE HOT WATER WITH CARE.

- NEVER RUN.

DESIGN SHEET 7

● On task Apply what you know

Discuss in groups the safety aspects of the dyeing process. If you make your own dyes, remember to be very careful – some dyes won't wash out. Consider the need for protective clothing. Write your ideas and conclusions on design sheet **7**.

On your design sheet

- Record your ideas about safety considerations for dyeing processes. **7**

Remember

- Synthetic dyes have more advantages than natural dyes but cause more damage to the environment.

All Stitched Up

How good are your sewing skills?
Do you need to practise a bit first
before you make your cushion cover?

If you haven't used a sewing machine
before, now is a good time to start.

Sewing machines

The first patent for a sewing machine was taken out
in 1790. However, it was not until the 1850s that
there were industrially made machines suitable for
use in the home. These were made by the Singer
Sewing Machine Company.

Domestic sewing machines can do about 1500
stitches in a minute. Industrial sewing machines
can do up to 5000 stitches in a minute!

Getting the tension right
The tension of your machine
must be balanced so that your
seam will not be too loose
or too tight.

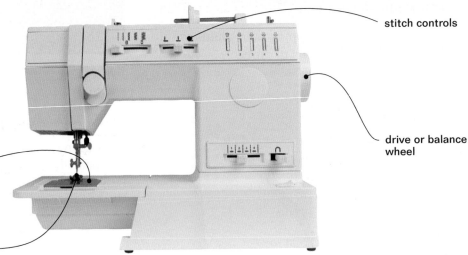

stitch controls

drive or balance
wheel

the feed dog
moves the
material along

needle

If the top thread is too loose
then the test sewing will look
like this.

If the top thread is too tight
then the test sewing will look
like this.

A well balanced stitch will look
like this. The top and bottom
threads lock in the fabric.

Some things to practise

1 A stitch in time

Always test the stitch on your sewing machine on a small sample of fabric. The stitch length, width and tension must be correct. This will avoid problems and having to waste time unpicking mistakes.

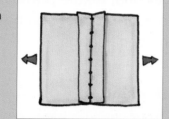

3 Making a hem on the back

It is important that the back pieces are hemmed neatly and straight.

To make a hem, turn under twice. Press with an iron. Stitch.

2 Inside out

Put the right sides of the fabric together. Make sure your seam allowances are 1cm.

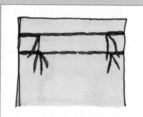

Practise sewing seams 1 cm apart. Remember to do a reverse at the end of each seam. This will give you stronger corners.

4 Tacking

Sometimes you need to tack pieces together before machine sewing. Tacking is a simple hand-stitch that holds the pieces in the correct position while machining. This avoids the fabric puckering.

DESIGN SHEET 8a

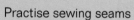

• Machine Testpieces

Stitch width 0
Stitch length 3
Reverse stitch at the end of each seam to prevent it unravelling.

Stitch width 4
Stitch length 3
Stitch width 2
Stitch length 4
Stitch width 1
Stitch length 1

Varying the width and length of the stitches alters the zig-zag.

● On task Apply what you know / Investigate

1. Practise your sewing techniques. Record the progress you made on design sheet **8a**.

2. Find out about the history of the sewing machine and how it works. Write what you discover on design sheet **8b**.

On your design sheets

- Explain what you did to practise your sewing skills. **8a**

- Record what you found out about the development of the sewing machine and how it works. **8b**

Remember

- Practising your sewing techniques will enhance the quality of your finished work.

Finishing Off

Your product will always be more successful if you have planned the making well first. The order in which you carry out tasks is very important.

How will you know whether your final textile product is successful or not? To evaluate your product you need to go back to your original design specification.

Planning the making

The following is a list of tasks to carry out to make your cushion cover. They are not in the right order.

▷ With a ruler and pencil, draw on the 1 cm seam allowance to use as a sewing guide.

▷ Hem the overlapping edges of both back pieces.

▷ Mark out the design on the front piece.

▷ Turn the cover right side out.

▷ Pin the backs to the front with the right sides together.

▷ Apply fabric paint to the front.

▷ Sew each side on the sewing machine. (Remember to reverse to strengthen the seams.)

▷ Overlock the edges to stop fraying.

▷ Iron the fabric when the paint is dry to fix the dye.

● On task 1 Plan the making

In groups, discuss the correct order for the tasks described above. Divide the order into two under the headings 'Painting the fabric' and 'Constructing the cushion cover'. Write your finished lists down on design sheet **9a**.

Making it!

● On task 2 Plan the making

1. Find out from your teacher exactly how many lessons you have available to make your product.

2. Plan out which tasks to do each week in order to complete your product in the time available. Show your plan on design sheet **9b**.

3. On design sheet **9b** write out lists of the tools and equipment you will need for:

▶ painting the design on the front

▶ constructing the cushion cover.

● On task 3 Work with materials

Get busy and start making your final cushion cover! Pay particular attention to the quality of your work. Keep checking to make sure everything is marked out accurately. Make sure your sewing is neat and straight. If it's not good enough you may need to re-do it.

Final evalution

To find out whether your final product is successful or not, go back to your original **design specification** (see page 34).

Criteria from design specification	Test	How successful?
1. Must co-ordinate with the Adinkra fabric by using similar colours and shapes.	survey	
2. Cover must fit a cushion of 32 x 32 cm.	try out	
3. Must be easy to take on and off the cushion pad so that it can be washed.	try out	
4. Design and making must be of good quality to attract buyers.	survey	

● On task 4 Final evaluation

1. In groups, evaluate your cushion cover. Use design sheet **9c**. Look at your fabric specification and test results, on design sheets **4a** and **4b**. Is the fabric you have used appropriate for a cushion cover?

> ▶ Criteria 2 and 3 can be tested by obtaining the correct sized cushion pad for your cover.

> ▶ Criteria 1 and 4 can be tested by asking others what they think.

2. Finally, on design sheet **9d** explain how you could improve the way you designed and/or made your cushion cover. Use **sketches** where possible.

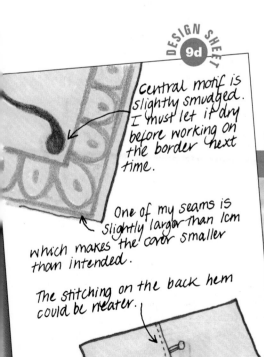

DESIGN SHEET 9d

Central motif is slightly smudged. I must let it dry before working on the border next time.

One of my seams is slightly larger than 1cm which makes the cover smaller than intended.

The stitching on the back hem could be neater.

On your design sheets

- Write down the correct order of making. **9a**
- Plan out the construction and write down the tools you will need. **9b**
- Test and evaluate your cushion cover. **9c**
- Suggest improvements to your work. **9d**

Remember

- Plan your work to get your product finished on time.
- Compare your final design with the design specification.
- Find out what other people think of your design.

An interview with...

Lesley Robinson is the Senior Design Co-ordinator at the CV Home Furnishings textiles design studio, in Swinton near Manchester.

If you want to learn more about CV Home Furnishings, go to:

www.technology.org.uk *Click on* **Industry**, *and then on* **Co–ordinated Bedroom Fabrics**.

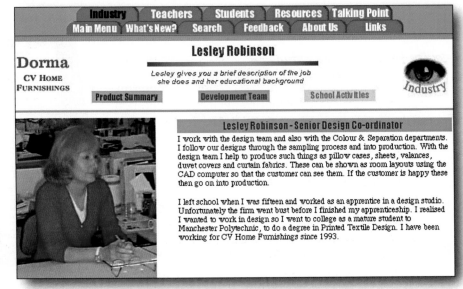

> " Here at CV Home Furnishings we design and make products such as duvet covers and curtains for bedrooms. These are co-ordinated so that, for example, curtain designs fit in with the design of duvet covers, pillow-cases, etc. We make the colours and patterns blend, match or contrast with each other to help the whole bedroom look good. "

What does your job involve?

> " My job is to make sure that a new design goes through the whole process smoothly. We start with a plan of development. This tells us all the tasks that have to be done and the time we are allowed for each task. Some tasks can be done alongside others. A good way to monitor our progress in this process is to create a special chart. This is called a *Gantt chart* and is put on the wall near where we work. "

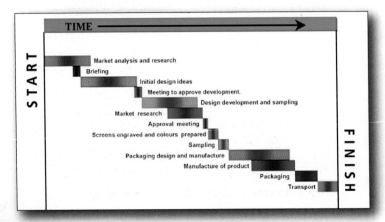

What influences your designs?

> " I discuss ideas with my design team and we prepare a concept board. This helps us to look at a variety of things that can influence the design. Influences can come from current fashion, from companies that forecast what people might want in the future and also from our own research. We also look very carefully at similar products from other companies already coming onto the market.
>
> From the concept board our designers develop several original artwork ideas. We then prepare these for a bed–linen fabric and for co-ordinating fabrics for curtains, valances, pillowcases, etc. These designs are developed and put onto design boards. We use these to display the ideas we have created to our customers. "

How are the designs developed?

" The next process is for the original artwork ideas to be scanned into the computer by our CAD specialist. Development at this point mainly involves creating the repeat pattern. This is where the size and shape of the design is adjusted so that it can be printed several times across the width and along the length of the chosen fabric.

CAD is also used to separate out each colour in the design. This is important for two reasons. First, we can work out how many colours of ink are needed. This tells us how many print screens are needed to print the design. Secondly we can try out different colour schemes using our basic design.

Once we are happy with a range of colours for the different designs, we print them onto real fabric by using a large inkjet printer. We turn these into samples of the articles we want to make from them. The client can then see how the finished curtains, pillow-cases etc., will actually look.

We also use the CAD system to put the designs onto a texture map of a bedroom. This is a wonderful way to give an instant impression of how a room would actually look if decorated using our design. "

How are the fabrics finally produced?

" At this stage the cost of production is worked out and we have a final meeting with the client so they can decide which designs they wanted us to manufacture.

Most of our designs are printed on a polyester and cotton mix fabric. This is because it is relatively cheap and has good wear and handling characteristics. Some of our more expensive designs are printed on pure cotton fabric which is more luxurious but much more expensive than polyester and cotton

mix fabrics. We select and assess new fabrics by using a series of tests. We have our own fabric testing department at our print works.

When all the fabric designs and colour schemes are decided and signed-off for production, the digital design files and the colour information are sent to the print works via a modem link.

The print factory sends the design files to a sub-contractor who makes the printing screens for each colour in the design. These screens are very large and expensive and many of them are needed for each design. It is vital that the designs are right at this stage because it would be too expensive to make the screens again. "

Room interiors created by CV Home Furnishings.

Starting Point

Museums and art galleries often run gift shops.
Visitors can buy souvenirs there to remind them of
their visit. Can you design and make a bag to sell
at an exhibition by the artist Matisse?

A local art gallery is
holding an exhibition of
the work of Matisse. The
director is looking for
products for the gift shop.

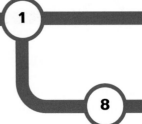

In a few months we will be holding an
exhibition of *papier collé* (paper cut-out)
work by the artist Matisse.

We would like to offer some souvenirs to
visitors that will remind them of the
exhibition. We expect visitors of all ages.
We are interested in small, simple bags
that are modern and colourful. They
should be decorated with an appliqué
panel that reflects the style of Matisse.

Creative Paper Society
Presents

Henri Matisse Cut-outs
30 January - 25 February

The Drawing Room Gallery
The Strand Quay
Sandstone, Kent

Opening Hours:
10:00 am - 5:00 pm
Telephone: 01304 123456
www.tdrg.co.uk

Admission: Free

◎ National Art Exhibitions

I will need the following
from you:

- initial ideas: sketches with notes suggesting colours,
  textures, patterns, shapes and techniques

- final idea, to include samples of intended materials

- a prototype of your final idea

- suggestions for other items we might sell, all based
  on the work of Matisse.

An Interview with...
Petra Boase

Hold Tight!

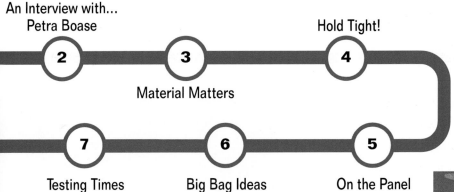

2 **3** **4**

Material Matters

7 **6** **5**

Testing Times   Big Bag Ideas   On the Panel

The focus

In this unit you will focus on really creative ideas, developing your designs and making an appliqué panel in the style of the artist Matisse.

The panel will be stitched onto a bag designed and made by yourself.

Henri Matisse

About Matisse

The artist Henri Matisse was born in France in 1869. He first started painting in the late 1880s, and continued until 1943 when an illness confined him to a wheelchair. At this point he began working on his 'paper cut-outs'. He used pre-coloured sheets of paper that he could cut into the shapes he wanted. He died in 1954.

The challenge

During this challenge you will use the work of Matisse as an inspiration for your designs. Looking at the work of the designer Petra Boase will help you do this.

You must investigate by looking at existing products and carrying out comparisons.

You will need to understand what appliqué is and how you do it.

The end product

Design and make a bag with an appliqué panel on the front. It must reflect the style of Matisse.

It's In The Bag

1

Cut it Out

How much do you know about bags and how they are constructed? Looking at the design of some existing bags will help you learn more.

What is product analysis?

Product **analysis** is a method used by designers and manufacturers. It involves studying an existing product to:

▷ see how it has been designed and made

▷ consider how it could be developed into a better product, or for a different market.

Sometimes it's possible to physically take a product apart, but this is not essential. With textile products a thorough examination will often do, though yarns and fabrics can be 'disassembled'.

In the bag

The basic idea of a bag is very simple. A bag enables someone to carry one or more objects more easily. There are many different types, from plain paper bags to designer handbags. The one you choose will depend on:

▷ the sort of things you want to carry

▷ where you are going

▷ what you are wearing

▷ who you will be with.

Metal handles and silver zips are a fashion detail rather than functional.

Clear side pocket allows you to label the bag.

A "weekend" bag. Suitable for carrying clothes, shoes etc. on short trips. Not strong enough for back packing.

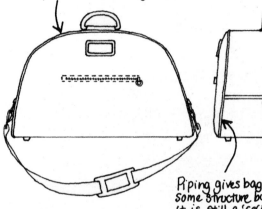

Piping gives bag some structure but it is still a 'soft' construction.

Strap can be used to carry the bag on the shoulder or removed with the metal clips

Dark colour will not show stains or dirt.

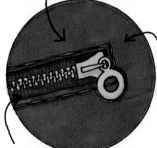

Medium/heavy plastic coated fabric makes the bag water proof.

Useful side, zip pocket provides a separate compartment for passports and papers.

● On task Evaluate

Find some examples of small, simple, modern and colourful bags to analyse.

In your group discuss the bags using the questions below to guide you. Try to make comparisons between the bags. For example:

'In this bag the handles have been sewn on, whereas in the other bag the handles are holes cut out of the sides.'

Analyse at least two different bags. Record your analysis on design sheet **1**. Make **sketches** of the bags (back, front and inside) and add notes.

▶ What things might usually be carried in this bag?

▶ Who might use this bag? When and where might it be used?

▶ What materials have been used? Have they been printed or dyed? How are they finished?

▶ Where are the seams, openings and so on?

▶ How has the bag been decorated?

▶ What fastenings and trimmings have been used?

▶ Are there any logos or labels?

▶ Has the bag been well designed and well made? Could it be improved in any way?

Remember

● Product analysis is a good starting point for designing. Looking at a range of similar products already on the market will give you more ideas.

On your design sheet

● Record your product analysis of a range of bags. **1**

An Interview with...

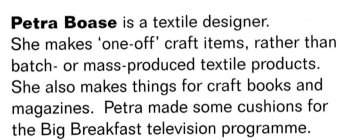

Petra Boase is a textile designer. She makes 'one-off' craft items, rather than batch- or mass-produced textile products. She also makes things for craft books and magazines. Petra made some cushions for the Big Breakfast television programme.

Where did you train, and what were your early influences?

❝ I started off doing a degree in embroidery at Manchester Metropolitan University. For my degree collection, I based my work on seaside 'finds'.

I like the way that using fabric for my work gives it texture. Although I do paint, I am frustrated by the flatness of the paint. When I create textile pictures, I think of it as using the needle as my brush. If I can't find the fabric I want, I create it by dyeing other fabric. ❞

What inspires you to create new pieces?

❝ Simple objects influence me, such as food packaging. For example after a trip to Vietnam I became inspired by the intense colours of the plastics in the markets.

I'm always looking for new sources of inspiration, and I like to travel and pick up ideas wherever I go.

I particularly like the Fauvist period in Art. It uses lovely bright colours and simple forms. Matisse was a Fauve. ❞

Curriculum Vitae
PETRA BOASE

DESIGNER, STYLIST, AUTHOR
BA HONS: Embroidery
Manchester Metropolitan
University

TELEVISION
ITV: *This Morning* (Granada)
BBC Choice: *Backstage* (Lion Television)

BBC 1: *Change That* (Bazal)

BBC 1: *Party of a Lifetime* (Bazal)

UK LIVING: *The Living Room* (Thames)

BOOK PUBLICATIONS

CONTRIBUTIONS TO BOOK PUBLICATIONS

On-screen interiors stylist/project maker. Live makeover of presenter's bedroom.
On-screen designer creating on the spot makeovers on pieces of junk furniture brought in by viewers.
On-screen designer, with Laurence LB, creating a middle-east themed party for 600 guests
On-screen designer creating DIY and style decorating trends.

Funky Junk, Carlton Books Ltd 1999
Nail Art for Kids, Carlton Books Ltd 1999
50 Christmas Craft for Kids, Lorenz Books 1998
Appliqué, Lorenz Books 1998
Creative Fun T-Shirt Painting, Lorenz Books 1997

The Colour Book, Laura Ashley
Inspirations Magazine series of themed books *Appliqué, Country Living*

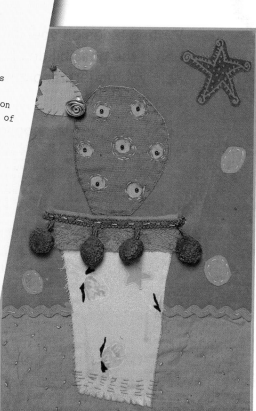

How do you start work?

66 When I first think of ideas for a new piece, I look at the doodles that I have done in my sketchbook. I adapt my doodles, because I love doodling and always keep a sketch book handy. Then when I start to develop my design, I play around with fabrics to get the right feel and colours.

I use lots of buttons, beads and lettering in my work. I do have a sewing machine but I don't use it much as my work is mainly done by hand. I like things to look spontaneous, and if I use the machine I think that makes it look more manufactured. 99

What other textile products do you design and make?

66 As well as the cushions for the Big Breakfast, and my 'makes' in books and magazines, I do work on commission. I make one-off framed pieces for private clients, who know and like the sort of work I do. 99

Hold Tight!

4

You are going to use appliqué as part of your bag. It is a good idea to practise the technique first.

Appliqué

Appliqué is a very old technique for decorating and embellishing fabrics. It involves applying one piece of fabric to another by machine or hand-stitching.

● On task 1 Investigate

Make a collection of scraps of fabrics to use for experimenting and designing. Remember the colours need to be similar to those used by Matisse for his *papier collé*. Include buttons and interesting yarns as well.

Holding the fabrics together

You need to hold your fabrics in the right position while you sew them. They must also be kept flat. There are three main ways of doing this: pinning, tacking and using adhesive.

Pinning the materials together is the simplest and quickest method, but **tacking** is more effective. Tacking is a simple hand stitch used to hold the fabric in position. Once you have stitched the fabric properly, the tacking can be taken out.

Sometimes **glue** is used to hold fabrics in place. The glue must not be too runny, or it might seep through to the right side of the fabric. A solid glue stick can be effective.

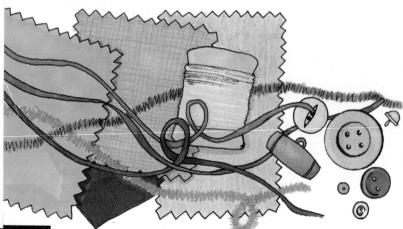

Bond-a-web is another possibility for holding fabrics in position. Bond-a-web:

▷ is especially good for items that are small or difficult to stitch

▷ is ideal for intricate outlines on flimsy material, as it adds structure and stiffness

▷ can stop materials from stretching

▷ prevents the fabric from fraying so there will be no need to turn under a seam allowance.

There are some disadvantages to using Bond-a-web though:

▷ it is not easy to re-position the fabric

▷ it is more expensive than tacking or pinning

▷ it can be very time consuming when used with many small, intricate pieces of fabric.

Using Bond-a-web

1 Cut out the fabric to the desired shape.

Cut out a piece of Bond-a-web the same shape.

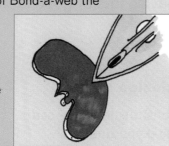

Examine the Bond-a-web closely. You will see that one side is paper and is very smooth. The other side is rough.

Beware – the rough side is glue. You must place your fabric on top of the glue side or the glue will stick to the iron in step 2.

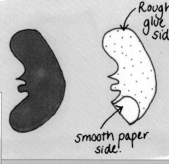

Rough glue side

smooth paper side!

2 Place the wrong side of the fabric on the glue, and iron. The glue will melt and stick to the wrong side of your fabric.

3 Allow to cool and peel the paper off the back. The glue is now on the fabric shape.

4 Place the fabric shape on your fabric background and iron. The glue will melt again and stick the shape to the background.

The fabric shape is now ready to embellish.

● On task 2 Work with materials

Cut out a shape and use one of the methods described here to hold it into a piece of background fabric. Use the sewing machine to sew. Apply some more scraps, and experiment with different lengths and widths of zig-zag stitch. Which stitch setting will look the neatest on your bag? Record the results of your investigation on design sheet **4**. Keep your appliqué sampler in your folder, and use it to test hand and machine stitches throughout the project (for example, on page 66).

On your design sheet

● Record how you held the fabric down on your appliqué sample. **4**

● Describe the different zig-zag stitches you used and record the stitch length and width of the best one. **4**

Remember

● Appliqué means applying one piece of fabric to another.

● Appliqué pieces can be held in position by pinning, tacking or by using adhesive.

On the Panel

5

You have completed your investigation. Now it is time to develop some design ideas for the appliqué panel. You need to start by having lots of good ideas.

'The Horse, the Squire and the Clown', Henri Matisse 1943–44

Techniques to help your design

There are many techniques that textile designers can use to develop design ideas. See if you find the following techniques useful.

1. Doodling

One of the best ways to come up with a variety of interesting ideas is to produce lots of quick, rough **sketches**. Add a few notes to help you remember what you were thinking at the time. Don't start to develop one idea in detail or draw any neat versions of a final design.

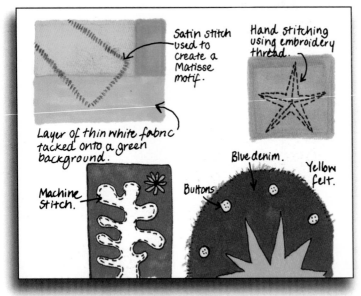

Satin stitch used to create a Matisse motif.

Hand stitching using embroidery thread.

Layer of thin white fabric tacked onto a green background.

Machine stitch.

Buttons

Blue denim.

Yellow felt.

● On task 1 Have good ideas

Read the interview with Petra Boase on pages 56 and 57 again. Try to design the way she does. Using the work of Matisse and Petra Boase as a resource, sketch quickly on design sheet **5a**. Draw all of your ideas as they come into your head. Remember, never use a ruler for freehand sketching.

2. Playing with materials

Handling and experimenting directly with the materials you will use is another method for having good ideas.

● On task 2 Have good ideas

Try designing using your fabric scraps. Move them around and try out different combinations and arrangements.

Make quick sketches on design sheet **5b** of the ideas you think work well.

3. Papier collé

When Matisse got old he was not able to paint so easily. Instead he got his assistants to paint sheets of paper in different colours. He then used them to cut out shapes with a pair of scissors.

Matisse arranged the shapes on a piece of background paper. When he felt his collage looked right it was stuck down.

⬤ On task 3 Have good ideas / Evaluate

1. Collect some scraps of coloured paper and try designing the same way that Matisse did. Keep your designs simple – use only two or three pieces of paper. Stick your designs down on design sheet **5c**.

2. Look back at all the ideas you have had. At the bottom of design sheet **5c**, say which methods helped you the most to come up with good design ideas.

On your design sheets

- Make quick sketches based on Matisse's work. **5a**

- Record what happened when you experimented with scrap materials. **5b**

- Create a series of *papier collé* designs. **5c**

Remember

- Drawing is not the only method for creating and trying out new ideas.

- It is always useful to experiment with fabrics and yarns.

- *Papier collé* is a technique used by Matisse.

Starting Point

Print IT Out

Cafés where people can use computers and access the Internet are becoming popular. Can you design and make some fabric designs for a new Internet café?

Getting on-line

Have you ever been to an Internet café? It's a place where you can buy coffee and other refreshments. At the same time you can use the café's computers to surf the Internet and e-mail friends.

Internet cafés first started to appear in the mid 1990s. At this time fewer people had access to computers and fast modems at home.

You have received the following e-mail.

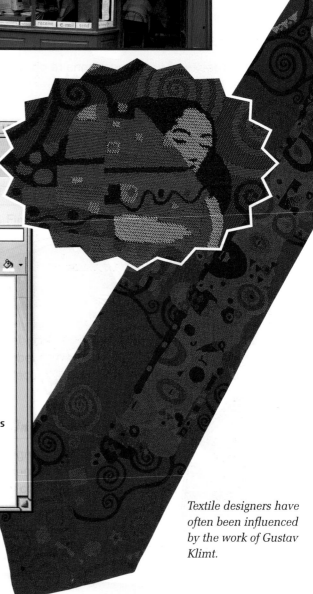

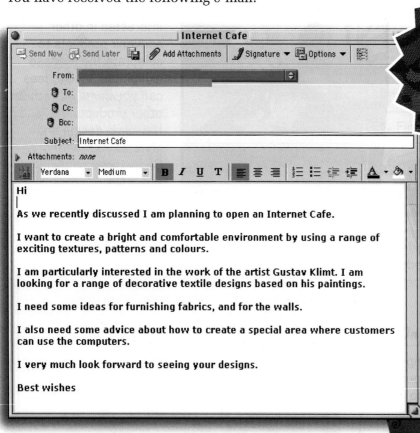

Internet Cafe

Send Now　Send Later　Add Attachments　Signature ▼　Options ▼

From:

To:

Cc:

Bcc:

Subject: Internet Cafe

Attachments: *none*

Verdana ▼　Medium ▼　**B** *I* U T

Hi

As we recently discussed I am planning to open an Internet Cafe.

I want to create a bright and comfortable environment by using a range of exciting textures, patterns and colours.

I am particularly interested in the work of the artist Gustav Klimt. I am looking for a range of decorative textile designs based on his paintings.

I need some ideas for furnishing fabrics, and for the walls.

I also need some advice about how to create a special area where customers can use the computers.

I very much look forward to seeing your designs.

Best wishes

Textile designers have often been influenced by the work of Gustav Klimt.

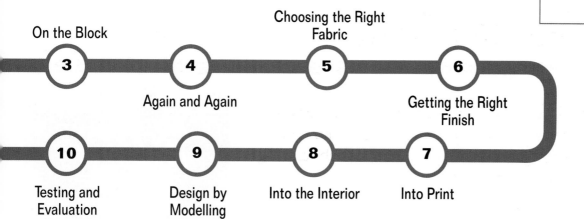

On the Block

3

4

Again and Again

Choosing the Right Fabric

5

6

Getting the Right Finish

10

9

8

7

Testing and Evaluation

Design by Modelling

Into the Interior

Into Print

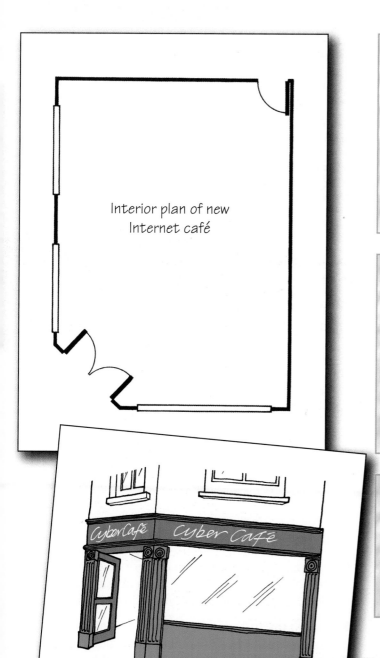

Interior plan of new Internet café

Cyber Café

The focus

In this unit you will focus on:

▶ producing a range of fabric and soft-furnishing designs for an Internet café using the work of the artist Gustav Klimt as your inspiration

▶ using **Information and Communication Technology** (ICT) to help you with your investigation and your designing.

The end product

You will need to produce a range of design ideas. These could be presented in book form, as presentation panels, or as a computer presentation.

At least one of your designs should be printed or stencilled on fabric. Some may be produced on paper. Some may be computer printouts.

The challenge

The challenge is to study the paintings of Gustav Klimt and create some designs of your own based on his style. You will use traditional techniques and computer technology to produce your designs.

Gustav Klimt

Print IT Out

The café must reflect the style of Gustav Klimt. First you will need to find out something about his life and work.

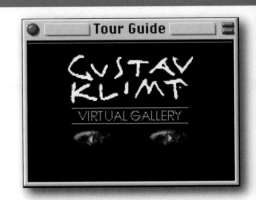

Finding out about Gustav Klimt

You may have come across the work of **Gustav Klimt** before. If you haven't, the information on these pages will give you an idea of:

▷ who he was

▷ where and when he worked

▷ the type of paintings he produced.

How can you find out more about him? To begin with you could look in the art section of your school or local library. Maybe your art department has its own books.

Remember it is visual research that will help you most with your designing. Don't write or print out too much written information.

As well as Klimt's paintings, find out about the furniture, jewellery, textiles and costumes of his period. This may give you more ideas. You could also find out more about other artists and designers of the period, such as C. R. Mackintosh, and Josef Hoffmann.

Searching on the Web

If your school has access to the Internet, or if you have access at home, you could use the World Wide Web to search for some information. You could use a **search engine** such as:

▷ **www.lycos.com**

▷ **www.altavista.com**

▷ **www.askjeeves.com**

Try entering key words such as **Gustav Klimt, Painting** or **Art Nouveau.**

Other websites, such as those belonging to museums and art galleries, might also have useful information.

Ask how you can either save the information you find, or print it out. Remember to make a note of the website address in case you want to go back to it again later.

You could also try searching CD-ROMs, such as Encarta or Britannica, or specialist History of Art CD-ROMs.

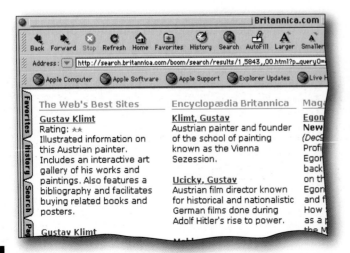

● On task 1 Investigate

1. On design sheet **1a** make a list of places where you are going to try to find out more about Gustav Klimt. Make some notes from the text on this page.

2. Record the further information you discover on design sheet **1b**. Remember to include pictures as well as words. These could be copied from books, computer printouts or simple **sketches** of your own.

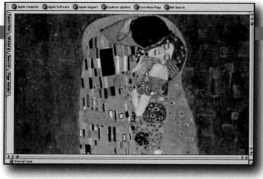

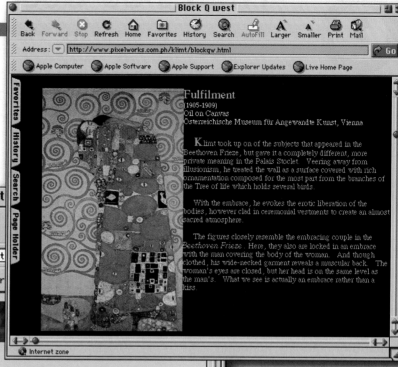

Fulfilment
(1905-1909)
Oil on Canvas
Österreichische Museum für Angewandte Kunst, Vienna

Klimt took up on of the subjects that appeared in the Beethoven Frieze, but gave it a completely different, more private meaning in the Palais Stoclet. Veering away from illusionism, he treated the wall as a surface covered with rich ornamentation composed for the most part from the branches of the Tree of life which holds several birds.

With the embrace, he evokes the erotic liberation of the bodies, however clad in ceremonial vestments to create an almost sacred atmosphere.

The figures closely resemble the embracing couple in the *Beethoven Frieze*. Here, they also are locked in an embrace with the man covering the body of the woman. And though clothed, his wide-necked garment reveals a muscular back. The woman's eyes are closed, but her head is on the same level as the man's. What we see is actually an embrace rather than a kiss.

WebMuseum, Paris

Klimt, Gustav

The work of the Austrian painter and illustrator **Gustav Klimt**, b. July 14, 1862, d. Feb. 6, 1918, founder of the school of painting known as the Vienna Sezession, embodies the high-keyed erotic, psychological, and aesthetic preoccupations of turn-of-the-century Vienna's dazzling intellectual world.

DESIGN SHEET 1c

● On task 2 Have good ideas

You have gathered lots of information about Klimt and his paintings. Now select some of his colours, textures, patterns and motifs that would make exciting fabric designs. Which ones would be suitable to make repeat patterns on a piece of fabric?

Explain and show your selections on design sheet **1c**.

On your design sheets

- Say where you plan to look for information about Klimt. **1a**
- Record what you discover. **1b**
- Explain which visual elements of Klimt's work you are going to base your designs on. **1c**

Remember

- The Internet provides access to information on a vast number of topics.
- Visual information is most important when investigating a theme.

What's So Good About IT?

Print IT Out

Using CAD (Computer Aided Design) has many advantages for the textile designer. How could you develop your designs for a fabric print using a computer system?

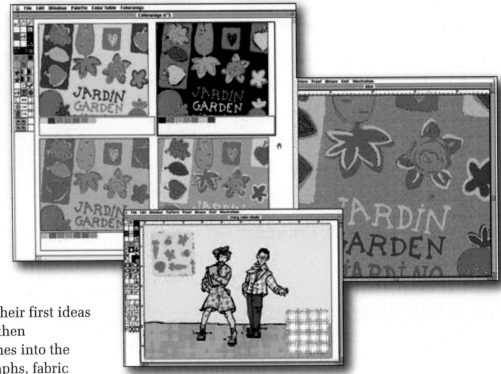

On screen

Textile designers use computers to develop and experiment with their ideas on screen. They can do this much more quickly than they can by hand. Their **design proposals** can then be printed out to show to a client.

Designers usually still sketch their first ideas on paper, however. They can then electronically scan their sketches into the computer, along with photographs, fabric samples and other artwork.

Time for change

A single shape can be re-sized, copied, rotated, mirrored, overlaid or distorted in seconds on screen. If the new version looks promising it can be saved for future reference. If not, there's a simple 'undo' button that restores the original design.

It's also easy to experiment with different colour combinations ('colourways'). The pattern and background can be set to any one of literally millions of colours, without mixing any paint. Again, if it doesn't look right, it only takes a moment to undo the change.

The design can then be printed out in colour onto paper, or onto special transfer paper and then ironed onto a piece of fabric. In industry, designs can be printed straight onto fabric.

Virtual reality textile products

Back on the computer, the design can be 'mapped' onto a framework of a 'virtual' fashion garment or room interior. This gives a good idea of what the fabric design will look like when made up into clothing or soft furnishings. The design can then be viewed in use in different settings and circumstances.

CAD–CAM

The electronic information about the design that exists in the computer can be used to give precise instructions to the machine that will print the fabric. This helps ensure that the shapes and colours come out looking exactly as the designer intended. The whole process of designing and making using a computer is known as **CAD–CAM** (**Computer Aided Design – Computer Aided Manufacture**).

Using IT in school

There are different ways you could use a computer in school to help you with your textile design work.

Using a scanner or digital camera

The **scanner** is like a large camera. It allows you to scan images (and text) directly into the software that you want to use. The images can be saved and used again and again.

You can also lay objects or fabrics onto the scanner. Take great care not to scratch the glass surface, though.

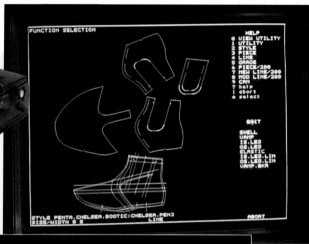

A **digital camera** is just like a real camera, except that the images are recorded electronically, instead of on film. If you connect a digital camera to a computer you can see your pictures on screen immediately.

A digital camera might be useful for taking electronic pictures as part of your investigation. You could also use it for recording designs you are developing.

Direct 2D design and drawing programs

There are a variety of different CAD programs available in schools. You might have some specialist textiles programs. Otherwise, use a **graphics**, **drawing** or **paint** package to explore shapes, textures and colours, and to create repeat patterns.

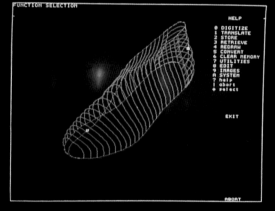

● *On task Investigate*

Find out what sort of scanners, cameras, printers and software programs are available in school to help you with your textile designing. Write down what you discover on design sheet **2**.

On your design sheet

- Make notes on what computers and programs you could use for designing textiles. **2**

Remember

- Hand-painted designs can be scanned into a computer. Then you can develop them quickly using different colours and repeats.

- Designs can be quickly and easily saved on disk.

Again and Again

4

Using a stencil is a good way to produce your designs on paper or fabric. Another method is called direct application. Can you use a variety of techniques and media to produce a really successful pattern design?

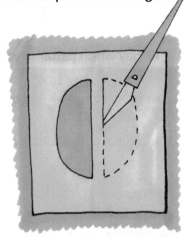

Stencilling

Stencilling involves cutting shapes from a piece of card. You place the stencil on the fabric and paint through the cut-outs with a special brush or sponge.

Cutting a stencil

To cut a stencil you will need:

▶ thin card or clear plastic
▶ a sponge or brush
▶ a craft knife
▶ a cutting board

How to stencil

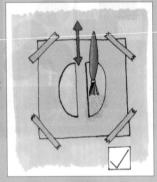

1 Apply the paint with a sponge or brush in an 'up and down' movement only. (The paint slips under the edge of the cut-out if a sideways movement is used.)

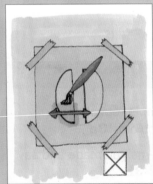

2 Use very little paint to start with. You can build up the colour in layers gradually. This will keep your work cleaner.

3 Keep the paint as dry as possible.

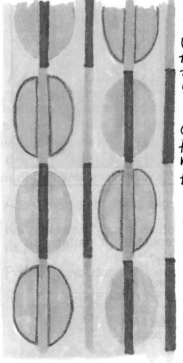

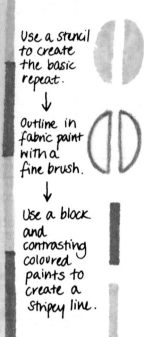

Use a stencil to create the basic repeat.

↓

Outline in fabric paint with a fine brush.

↓

Use a block and contrasting coloured paints to create a stripey line.

● On task 1 Apply what you know

Select one of the motifs you picked out from Klimt's paintings. Make your own stencil of it using thin card or plastic. Use your stencil to create some repeat patterns on some suitable fabric or paper. Mount this on design sheet **4a**.

Combining techniques

Your design may be too complex to be produced from one block or one stencil. This problem is easily solved. You can:

▷ use two or three blocks

▷ use a block and a stencil

▷ combine blocks and stencils with a **direct application** method.

Direct application

Direct application means applying colour directly onto the fabric using fabric paints, fabric crayons and fabric pens.

Fabric paints can be used to apply areas of colour. Sponging the paint on will create a textured effect.

Fabric crayons will give bold lines. When used on their sides they give a rough textured effect.

Fabric pens can be used for adding fine lines and details.

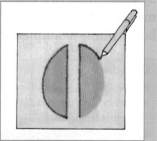

Using CAD

On a computer you can use a **masking tool** in a paint or graphics programme to create and experiment with ideas for stencils. These can then be printed out.

Many graphics programs have a range of different types of textured surfaces and crayon, pen and brush types that can be applied.

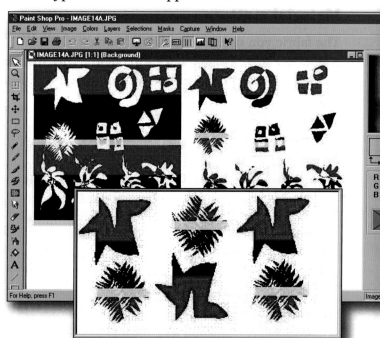

● On task 2 Have good ideas

Try using a two or three blocks, a block and a stencil, or a combination of techniques to produce a more complex repeat in the style of Klimt. Work on paper with pens and paints. Mount this work on design sheet **4b**.

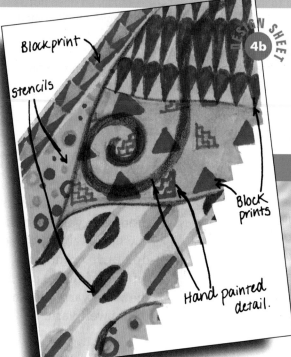

Blockprint

stencils

Block prints

Hand painted detail.

On your design sheets

- Make and use a stencil based on Klimt's paintings. **4a**
- Use a combination of techniques to make a complex repeat pattern in the style of Klimt. **4b**

Remember

- There are many ways of applying colour to fabric.
- Stencils and blocks produce repeat designs.

Testing and Evaluation

10

Print IT Out

What will the owner of the Internet café think of your designs for the interior and textiles? You need to prepare a presentation of your work.

Then it will be time to evaluate your final product, process and presentation.

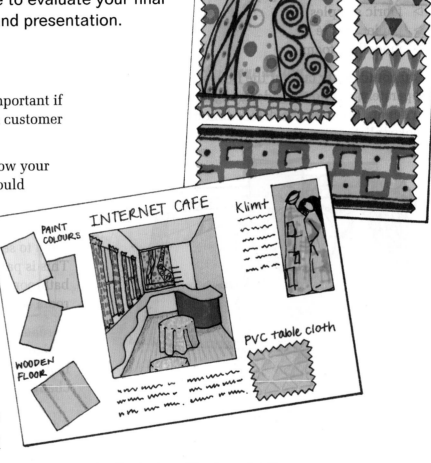

Presentation matters

The way you present your ideas is very important if you are a designer. It can help persuade a customer to buy your designs.

There are a number of ways you could show your work. To complement your model, you could produce:

▷ a book of fabric samples

▷ a mood board

▷ a display panel

▷ a computer presentation.

What was wanted?

The owner of the Internet café made the following points. The interior had to:

▷ use textiles to help create a bright and comfortable atmosphere

▷ have a special area for computers

▷ include furnishing fabrics that reflect the style of Gustav Klimt.

Plan your presentation to show as clearly as possible that you have achieved all these things.

● On task 1 Develop your design

Decide how you will present your ideas. Make notes on design sheet **10a**.

● On task 2 Final evaluation

In your group discuss whether you achieved all of the café owner's criteria. Present your ideas to each other.

▶ Briefly explain how your designs developed and how they reflect the works of Klimt. How well does your print reflect Klimt's style?

▶ Clarify how your print could be used to make the computer area bright and attractive.

▶ How could your fabric be mass-produced?

Record your evaluation on design sheet **10b**.

● On task 3 Final evaluation

What ideas have you got for improvements? These could be improvements for the designs or suggestions for improving your printing technique. How many of the following did you manage to achieve?

▶ Motifs evenly spaced?

▶ Attractive textural effects using sponge and wooden blocks?

▶ Clean edges around stencils?

▶ Paint applied evenly?

▶ Details applied well with pens?

▶ Overall professional finish?

Record your suggestions for improvements on design sheet **10b**.

● On task 4 Final evaluation

How were you able to use the Internet for investigation, or any other computer applications to help develop your design? On design sheet **10c** write a short report on what you did using ICT and how this improved your design work. Suggest some advantages and disadvantages of using ICT in school and in industry.

Taking into account what those surveyed said about my textiles print and presentation, I would make the following improvements:
1. Put a little less information on my display panel to make it easier for people to see.
2. Try to apply fabric paint more evenly. It works better if I start by using a small amount of paint and then building it up in layers. This avoids putting too much on which makes blobs and smudges. This will give a more professional result.
3. Make more use of fabric pens to add details rather than trying to apply them with a brush.

On your design sheets

● Explain how you plan to present your work. **10a**

● Record what other people said about your designs. **10b**

● Say what improvements you would like to make. **10b**

● Describe how you used ICT. **10c**

Remember

● To be really successful, your product should match the original specification.

● Always seek other opinions, from friends or experts, as they will sometimes see things in a different way.

An Interview with...

Print IT Out

Lucy Wright is Development Manager for Penn Nyla. Penn Nyla is a knitted fabric manufacturer producing textiles for customers making lingerie, active sportswear and car seats. These fabrics are used by many major international brand names.

Lucy is responsible for producing the new fabrics that its customers need to sustain their businesses. Her work covers the full development process.

This involves:

▷ initial discussions with customers or salespeople
▷ designing the fabric
▷ prioritising the work
▷ supervising the knitting and processing
▷ assessing the finished product.

After analysing the structure of a fabric, Lucy then prepares a development specification.

How does a new product get started?

❝ New products generally start in one of two ways. It might be something thought up by our sales, development and design teams. They are constantly trying to create new ideas to sell in our competitive markets.

Alternatively it might be in response to a specifc request from a customer. In this case the customer will normally give us a fairly precise brief to work to. Our first ideas may be sketchy, especially if the concept is a very new one.

I then produce a knitting specification from this request, taking into account cost (always important), the various yarns we have at our disposal and the capabilities of our knitting and dyeing machines.

We frequently cost out a product before making it to ensure it fits the customer's cost requirement and also allows us to make a profit. ❞

What performance tests are carried out on new fabrics?

66 This depends on the final use of the fabric. It is often defined by the customer or our knowledge of the usage.

For example, car seating fabrics are subject to very severe abrasion tests and light-fastness tests to ensure that they do not wear out or fade.

Lingerie fabrics usually incorporate elastane yarns for stretch. Stretch and recovery properties are important for fit and comfort, as well as colour–fastness when washing.

With active sportswear, stretch may also be important but the wicking properties of the fabric, which enable it to transfer sweat to the atmosphere and keep the wearer cool, are often paramount for sports such as football and athletics. 99

How is ICT used?

66 We use ICT in the development process, both for communication of specifications between the development team and for product design.

We have systems that help us to design and visualise stitch constructions and dedicated CAD systems for the electronic jacquard machines. We also use a specification database to calculate fabric weights and costs and to archive full specifications of existing products. This can then be used to search for a fabric to meet a customer's requirements or to give us a starting point for a new one. 99

What have some of your most successful products been?

66 In active sportswear we were very successful in the introduction of microfibres into football shirts to give better wicking and greater comfort. With the use of jacquard technology we can now knit mesh ventilation panels into the garments without the need for stitching. This has developed into a multi-million pound business.

In lingerie we have also capitalised on the latest electronic jacquard machines to produce stretch fabrics with sophisticated patterns and iridescent effects while still giving good fit and comfort.

We have also successfully introduced "Coolmax" (a special fibre for wicking away perspiration) into sports underwear, in fabrics which also give good support. This is technology that we have transferred from our sportswear business. 99

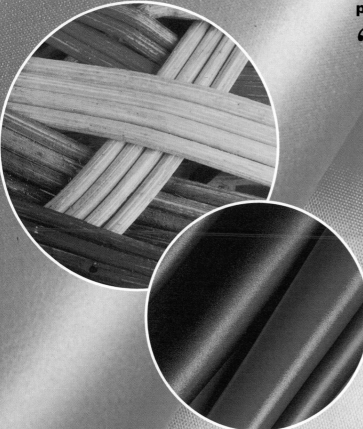

Starting Point

Get ahead

Get a hat!

Can you design and make a hat to be worn by people on an adventure holiday?

Going off on an adventure

Many people choose to go on holidays that offer activities. Walking holidays at scenic locations are increasingly popular.

You have received the following letter from Adventure Holidays Ltd.

Dear Designer,

I represent Adventure Holidays Ltd. We specialise in walking holidays to various mountainous locations across Europe. We cover rough terrain and the weather conditions can be hazardous and unpredictable.

With the expansion of our company we are seeking to establish a clearer identity for ourselves by adopting a new logo. This will be used on our next range of leisure wear, including T-shirts, sweatshirts and hats.

We would like you to design and produce a prototype for a hat. The hat will be worn by our expedition leaders and those participating in our adventure holidays.

The hat should:

- identify the wearer to the rest of the group when fog, mist and rain descend
- be adaptable to suit different weather conditions
- be lightweight so it can be carried easily.

Adventure Holidays' current brochure and logo

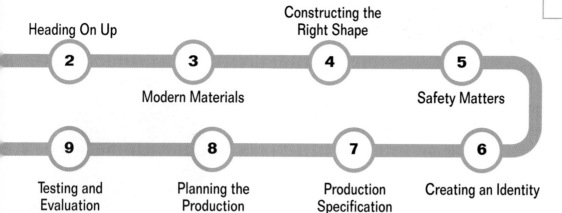

Heading On Up
2

3
Modern Materials

Constructing the
Right Shape
4

5
Safety Matters

9
Testing and
Evaluation

8
Planning the
Production

7
Production
Specification

6
Creating an Identity

The challenge

The challenge is to design and make a hat. The hat needs to be suitable for mountain walking in changeable weather conditions.

You also need to create a simple logo to go on the hat.

The focus

In this unit you will have to:

▶ investigate and choose appropriate fabrics

▶ use product **analysis** to find out how different hat designs are constructed.

The end product

You will need to produce:

▶ an outdoor hat that is lined and displays the Adventure Holidays logo

▶ a range of design ideas for other Adventure Holidays garments.

People in Hats

1

Get ahead

Get a hat!

Throughout history people have worn headwear for many different reasons.

Using the right headwear

Hats are worn for:

protection
decoration
safety
hygiene
fun
identity
worship

● On task 1 Investigate

Look at each headwear illustration on page 96.

► Where and why is each hat worn?

► Describe the materials needed to make each hat.

► What is the **function** of each hat?

Record your **analysis** on design sheet **1a**.

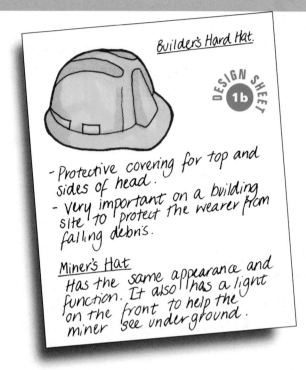

Builder's Hard Hat.

DESIGN SHEET 1b

- Protective covering for top and sides of head.
- Very important on a building site to protect the wearer from falling debris.

Miner's Hat
Has the same appearance and function. It also has a light on the front to help the miner see underground.

● On task 2 Investigate

In groups, carry out a survey into what hats are popular today.

► When and where do people wear hats?

► Do you know anyone who has been on a walking holiday? Talk to some people who wear hats as part of their job, or when out walking. Ask them about their most important needs in terms of headwear and clothing.

► Visit shops and look through magazines and catalogues to find out what kinds of hats are available for outdoor wear. What materials are they made from and how much do they cost?

Record the findings from your survey on design sheet **1b**. **Sketch** some of the outdoor hats you found out about and mount any pictures you found. Label the materials, prices and particular design features. You could use a **spreadsheet** to complete a group comparison.

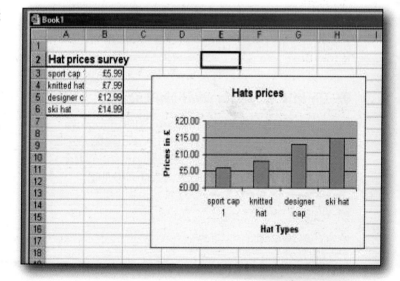

On your design sheets

● Use notes and sketches to describe the hats shown on these pages. **1a**

● Record the findings of your survey. Sketch and label any hats you found out about. **1b**

Remember

● Hats are worn for many different reasons.

● Investigating these reasons, old and new, will help you think of more ideas for your hat design.

Heading On Up

Get ahead

Get a hat!

Focus carefully on what you are being asked to do.
Then you can start to develop some first design ideas
for your hat.

SPEEDO®

Who will use your hat?

Who likes to go on walking holidays?

▷ men and women

▷ all age groups, from teenagers to OAPs.

Ergonomics is the study of the way that a product,
the user and the environment affect each other.

When designing your hat, think carefully about the
health, safety, convenience and comfort of the user.
Consider carefully the environment in which the
product will be worn.

● *On task 1 Apply what you know*

Read the letter from the manager of Adventure
Holidays on page 94 again. Write a **design
specification** for the hat on design sheet **2a**.
Make clear statements about the following.

▶ Who is it for?

▶ What is it for?

▶ When will it be worn?

▶ What sort of weather conditions might the hat
have to withstand?

▶ What sort of safety features will the hat need
to have?

● *On task 2 Investigate / Evaluate*

Make a collection of logos used by a range of sports
and adventure clothing companies. Stick or copy them
onto design sheet **2b**. Add notes to explain how they
work, and evaluate them. Discuss their shape, colour
and style of lettering.

● *On task 3 Have good ideas*

On design sheet **2c sketch** your first ideas for your
hat and some logos for Adventure Holidays.

Using CAD

Use a **computer-aided design** package to explore ideas for the colours and shapes of the hat and the logo.

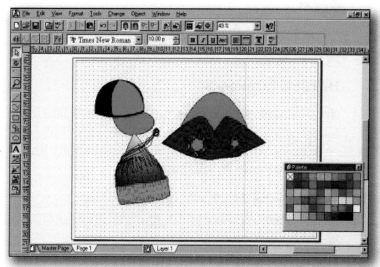

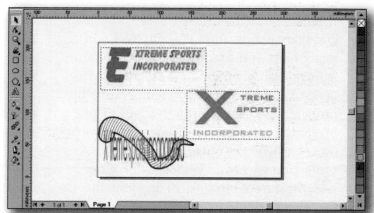

DESIGN SHEET 2a

fleece.

Stretch ribbed fabrics

The fastening could be ties or buttons.

Drawstring fleece hat.

Sun protection from a peak at the front.

Reflective strip.

Logo.

Hood with built-in sun visor and Velcro strap fastening.

Protective shell with soft/warm lining.

On your design sheets

- Create a design specification for the hat. **2a**
- Record your study of sportswear logos. **2b**
- Sketch hat and logo ideas. **2c**

Remember

- Writing specifications will help you focus on what is required of you.

Modern Materials

Get ahead

Get a hat!

Consider what sort of materials would be best for your hat. Then you can develop and finalise your design.

Guaranteed To Keep You Dry

GORE-TEX® outerwear

GORE Creative Technologies Worldwide

Ocean technology

Hi-tech fabrics

Great advances have been made in **hi-tech fabrics** in recent years. The most recent technology can combine warmth with lightness, breathability and water repellence in one fabric.

Smart materials are able to change their **properties and characteristics**, depending on their environment.

Cold, wind and rain

Our body temperature is about 37°C. In many parts of the world the air temperature is lower than that. So in these places we need to maintain our body temperature by protecting ourselves from the cold. The bigger the temperature difference between ourselves and the outside, the more protection we need. We lose a lot of our body heat from our head. Therefore, the **function** of the hat you are designing, to trap in the heat, is extremely important.

Water repellence with breathability – keeping dry

Traditionally, waterproof fabrics coated with oil or resin allowed no escape route for perspiration so it turned to water on the skin, making the wearer very uncomfortable.

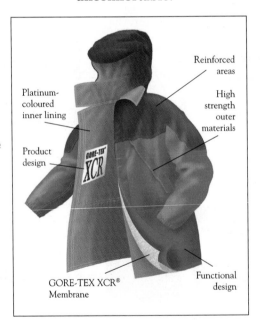

Platinum-coloured inner lining

Product design

Reinforced areas

High strength outer materials

GORE-TEX XCR® Membrane

Functional design

Breathable fabrics actually conduct body perspiration to the outer surface along a chain of hydrophilic (water-attractive) molecules. At the same time the fabric remains waterproof and impervious to exterior weather conditions. **GORE-TEX®** is an example of a breathable fabric.

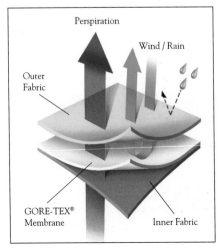

Perspiration

Wind / Rain

Outer Fabric

GORE-TEX® Membrane

Inner Fabric

● *On task 1 Investigate*

1. Use a range of sources to investigate the most recent innovations in hi-tech and smart textile materials. Look at the labels on garments in shops and descriptions in catalogues. Record what you discover on design sheet **3**.

2. Find out from your teacher what fabrics are available in school. You may need to use cheaper versions of hi-tech fabrics for your hat, such as waterproof nylon and brushed cotton.

Warmth with lightness – keeping warm

Polartec is a lightweight fabric that enables you to control your 'body climate'. This helps you stay comfortable, regardless of the weather or activity. Polartec is a knitted fabric that fits comfortably and stretches with the body. It is also brushed, which means extra air is trapped between the raised fibres. Air is a good insulator, so this helps maintain body warmth. Polartec is designed to be the middle or outer layer of an outdoor garment, and provides warmth without weight.

● On task 2 Apply what you know

Add in a fabric specification to your hat **design specification** on design sheet **2a**. State clearly what **properties and characteristics** the fabric will need to have. (See page 98.)

Using ICT

You can use the Internet to find out how modern fabrics are made and marketed.

• Textile Innovations

Sources of information:
Internet : I printed out some interesting articles from fabric manufacturers, websites.

Magazines : Our local library had some specialist magazines that contained information on current and future innovations.

Shops : Sports clothes often have labels that describe the innovations used to create the garment.
    I picked up some catalogues made by Gore-tex and Polartec that contained useful diagrams of how these fabrics work.

On your design sheets

● Record what you discover about recent textile innovations. Say where you found your information. **3**

● Add a fabric specification to your design specification. **2a**

Remember

● Technology is used to develop fabrics with particular properties.

● The more air that can be trapped between fabric layers and fibres the warmer the clothing will be.

● Air is a good insulator.

Constructing the Right Shape

Get ahead

Get a hat!

It isn't easy making a hat. Studying some existing hats will help you to understand how they work.

Then you need to start thinking about the pattern pieces you will need.

Product analysis

Designers always carry out an **analysis** of the products that are already on the market. They can find out how they are made and improve on them.

HOOD PATTERN

Side panel.

Back panel.

Hanging hook

Logo.

Front panel.

DESIGN SHEET **4a**

Adjustable fabric strip with velcro to allow tightening of cuff to stop wind and rain. I could use this detail on my designs.

This rip stop fabric is waterproof and strong.

Double top stitch makes the seam strong and waterproof.

Quilted lining contains wadding that gives added warmth.

Polyester netting is used inside the back of the jacket to aid ventilation through the vent.

HOOD FASTENINGS

Velcro patch.

Adjustable strap.

elastic cord.

zip

Metal eyelet.

Vent.

The versatile hood design can be tightened around the face with elastic cord and locks.

The jacket fastening is very functional. The zip is covered by a wind flap fixed by velcro squares.

● On task 1 Investigate / Evaluate

Carry out a product analysis of a hat that was designed and made for outdoor wear. What were the user needs of the wearer of this hat? Do you think that this hat fulfilled its **function**? Record your study on design sheet **4a**. Add colour to show texture and pattern. Use notes to describe and comment on the design.

If you cannot find a hat, try looking at a windbreaker or anorak instead. Use the examples on these pages to help you.

Round or rectangular?

Experiment to work out suitable **pattern** pieces to make a hat that fits the crown of a person's head. One approach is to try a circular shape, another a rectangular shape. The one you choose depends on the type of hat you are designing.

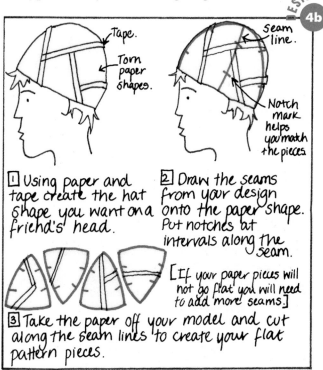

Using ICT

If you have a pattern drafting program you could use it to develop your pattern pieces. The patterns can be printed out at quarter, fifth or half size, or at full scale.

You could also use the program to experiment with the layout of the pieces on the material. This will reduce the amount of wastage. At the same time you can estimate how much fabric you will need for making one hat, or for a batch of hats.

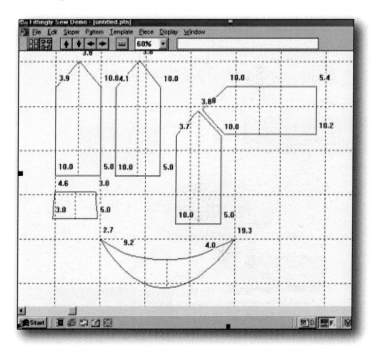

● On task 2 Develop your design

1. In pairs, cut some pattern pieces out of paper and try fitting them around your partner's head. Make a shape to fit the crown of the head. This could be a circle or a rectangle.

2. Place the paper on your partner's head. How does it fit?

3. How can you cut or manipulate the paper to develop the pattern?

4. On design sheet **4b**, make notes on how these pattern pieces could be finalised for your hat design.

5. What differences will using woven or knitted fabric make to the sizes of your pattern pieces?

On your design sheets

● Make a detailed study of an outdoor garment. **4a**

● Record your suggestions for pattern pieces. **4b**

Remember

● Understanding existing products will enrich and improve the quality of your design.

● Experimenting with pattern pieces will give you a deeper understanding of hat construction.

Safety Matters

Get ahead

Get a hat!

Take your design a stage further by sorting out some details. Have you taken safety into account?

Experimenting with pattern pieces will have given you ideas for the basic construction of your hat.

Getting down to detail

▷ How will you make sure the hat stays on?

▷ What type of fastening will your intended user find easiest to use?

▷ How can you make your hat safer?

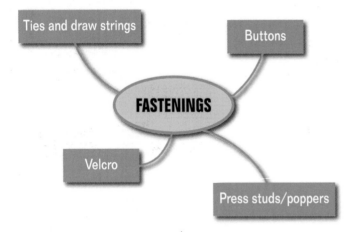

Ties and draw strings

Buttons

FASTENINGS

Velcro

Press studs/poppers

3M™ Scotchlite™ reflective material

3M invented reflective materials over 50 years ago. The materials are made from millions of tiny glass lenses with a mirror coating that reflects light back to its source. They have been widely used for safety wear to increase the visibility of the wearer at night. Since then 3M have developed new reflective materials that have expanded the range of potential applications of their products in new markets.

3M recently developed a new material that reflects brilliant white when illuminated by artificial light at night (for example car headlights). As well as clothing, the new fabric can be used for things like logos, gloves and shoelaces. Apart from the potential benefit to cyclists and pedestrians, the fabric also has the possibilities for fashion wear. The new fabric consists of high performance glass lenses bonded onto a polyester/cotton backing. It is resistant to abrasion and chemicals, highly durable, and can be washed at home or dry-cleaned.

3M also now offer a range of coloured reflective inks that create dazzling reflected images when screen-printed on cotton, cotton blends and absorbent fabric finishes. They are used for fashion and leisure wear and for promotional clothing. The inks are available in seven colours – silver, blue, green, red, white, orange and yellow. Multicolour printing creates stunning images and pigments can be mixed with silver. After printing a fabric, a water-repellent treatment can be applied.

● On task 1 Develop your design

Read about the 3M Scotchlite reflective fabric, on the right.

In groups, discuss the benefits of various safety features such as fluorescent strips (reflectors).

► Which safety features would be right for your hat?

► Which features would be safest? Which would be most convenient?

Make notes of the points you have discussed on design sheet **5a**.

● On task 2 Develop your design

On design sheet **5b** sketch some more ideas, taking into account safety features. Label the various design features on each sketch.

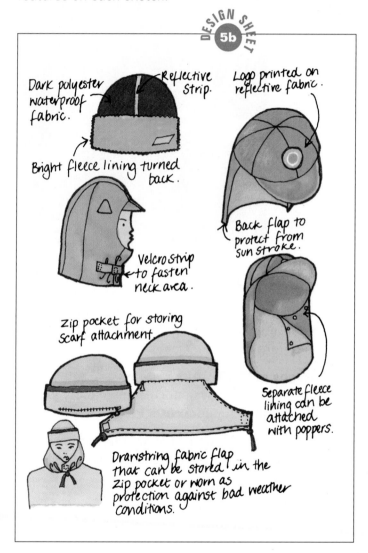

DESIGN SHEET 5b

Dark polyester waterproof fabric.

Reflective Strip.

Logo printed on reflective fabric.

Bright fleece lining turned back.

Back flap to protect from sun stroke.

Velcro strip to fasten neck area.

Zip pocket for storing scarf attachment.

Separate fleece lining can be attached with poppers.

Drawstring fabric flap that can be stored in the zip pocket or worn as protection against bad weather conditions.

Final design

Look carefully at all your ideas.

▷ Which design can you develop further to take forward as your final product?

▷ Which design best meets the criteria of your **specification**?

▷ How can you improve it so that it meets the specification more fully?

● On task 3 Develop your design

Prepare a neat **presentation** drawing of your final improved design on design sheet **5c**. Explain why this is the best design. Show on your presentation drawing where you will stitch the logo. It can be designed in more detail later.

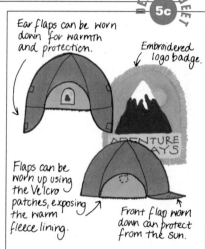

DESIGN SHEET 5c

Ear flaps can be worn down for warmth and protection.

Embroidered logo badge.

Flaps can be worn up using the Velcro patches, exposing the warm fleece lining.

Front flap worn down can protect from the sun.

On your design sheets

- Make notes from your discussion. **5a**
- Sketch out your ideas and label them. **5b**
- Present your final design, explaining why it is best. **5c**

Remember

- Some fastenings will be easier and therefore safer, to use than others in different situations.
- Safety features are necessary for many types of outdoor clothing.
- Careful design of details and finishing touches will make your textile product stand out against the competition.

Creating an Identity

Get ahead

Get a hat!

Adventure Holidays need a logo that will be easily identifiable to its customers and the general public. Can you design and make a logo that can be attached to your hat?

What are logos and symbols?

Organisations use **logos** and **symbols** to help customers quickly recognise them. Logos and symbols should be simple and have an immediate impact.

A logo contains the name of the company or its initials (see examples on pages 98 and 99). A symbol is a shape or illustration, which may represent some aspect of products or services offered by the company. A logo and symbol are often combined together into one design.

You have already sketched some designs for logos or symbols.

● On task 1 Develop your design

Look back at design sheet **2c** at the first ideas you had for logo designs. On design sheet **6a** develop these further and in more detail.

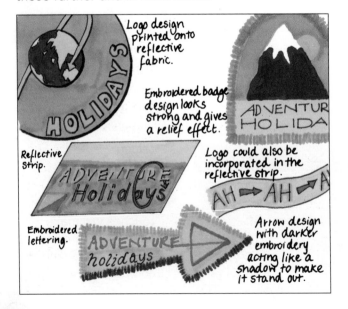

Logo design printed onto reflective fabric.

Embroidered badge design looks strong and gives a relief effect.

Reflective strip.

Embroidered lettering.

Logo could also be incorporated in the reflective strip.

Arrow design with darker embroidery acting like a shadow to make it stand out.

ADVENTURE HOLIDA

AH ➤ AH ➤ A

ADVENTURE holidays

Using CAD–CAM

In industry, logos and badges are made using **CAD** (**computer-aided design**), and **CAM** (**computer-aided manufacture**).

Advantages of CAD–CAM systems
▷ Using a computer system cuts down on labour and time and therefore costs less.

▷ CAM produces designs that are identical and therefore there is a greater consistency of quality.

Disadvantages of CAD–CAM systems
▷ You may be limited to the number of colours you can use in your logo.

▷ The machine may operate within a size limit.

In CAD-CAM systems, there must be an **input** (the design) that is **processed** to produce an **output** (the product).

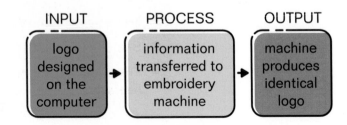

INPUT	PROCESS	OUTPUT
logo designed on the computer	information transferred to embroidery machine	machine produces identical logo

CNC (Computer numerical control)

A CNC machine incorporates its own computer that can be programmed to make specific components. CNC machines are often used as part of complex automated production systems. They are particularly effective where a small manufacturer specialises in the making of a component that is part of the whole product, such as labels or embroidered logos.

CAD–CAM in school

You may have some facilities for using CAD–CAM in school, such as a computer-generated embroidery machine on which you could design and manufacture your logo. However, there will be limitations to the designs you can make using such a system. For example, there will be a size limit and a limit to the number of colours that can be used.

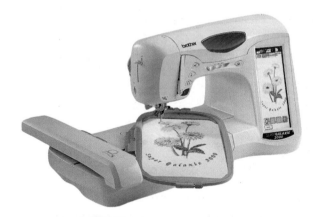

If CAD–CAM is not available, consider using other techniques to help you design and make your logo. For example, you could use appliqué or embroidery.

Buying it in

A manufacturer may not make all the parts of a product. Some items, such as an embroidered logo or labels, will be 'bought in' from another specialist manufacturer. They are then incorporated with the product during manufacture by being fused onto it, or sewn into the product seam.

Fixing it on

How will the logo be attached to your hat? You could use Bond-a-web or a fabric glue, or an embroidery stitch.

DESIGN SHEET 6b

I have decided to machine embroider the logo onto my hat. Embroidery gives a good quality finish and will make the badge very secure.

● On task 2 Develop the design / Plan the making

On design sheet **6b** produce a drawing of your final design for a logo. Describe the possibilities for using CAD–CAM in your school. Alternatively, describe what other means you will use to make your design and to fix it to your hat.

On your design sheets

- Develop your design for the logo for your hat. **6a**

- Finalise your design, and say how you are going to make it. **6b**

Remember

- Logos and symbols help create an identity for a company.

- CAD–CAM systems save on labour and time and therefore costs.

- Using CAM produces identical, high quality designs.

Production Specification

Get ahead

Get a hat !

In industry, when a final design has been completed a production specification is drawn up. This helps ensure the quality of a product.

Can you write a production specification for your hat design, and work out how much it would cost to make in quantity?

Production specification

A **production specification** is completed before a product is batch- or mass-produced. This provides all the technical details about the product. It is given to the people who will manufacture the product. This helps ensure that the products are all identical, and of the required quality.

● *On task 1 Plan the making*

1. Draw up a production specification for your product on design sheet **7a**.

2. Write a materials list and an equipment list on design sheet **7b**.

Production specification

Sketch

General information

Logo to be attached to centre front panel

Join outer components

Attach reflector strip *

Join lining components

Insert care label and other label between two lining components

Attach Velcro to ear-flaps *

Join lining to outer hat inside out

Turn through

Finish off *

*Quality control points

Components	Materials
4 head panels	100% nylon outer fabric
2 ear flaps	100% cotton lining fabric
in outer fabric and in lining fabric	

Trimmings	Thread
Velcro	60' polysew
fluorescent reflective strip	
logo	

Stitch size	Seam allowance
length 3 width 0	1 cm on all components

Care label	Other labels
[40] ⊠ ⊠ ⊠ ⊙ DO NOT BLEACH	Shell 100% NYLON Lining 100% COTTON KEEP AWAY FROM FIRE MADE IN ENGLAND

Costing your product

How much would it cost to make your hat? To calculate this you will need to work out the total amount of materials and components required.

Adventure Holidays will want to make many more than one hat, however. How much would it cost to make 100 hats? How much to make 10,000?

● On task 2 Plan the making

1. Use trade catalogues to find prices for the materials and components you would need. Remember things are usually cheaper if you buy in bulk. Don't forget to include delivery to your workshop!

2. Work out the cost of the materials needed for making 500 hats. Record the data you find, and your calculations, on design sheet **7c**.

Making it all add up

For the costing task, you were not asked to include the costs of labour, energy, packaging, transport, VAT, and a whole variety of other costs involved in making a product in quantity. In fact the cost of the materials is often less than 10% of the price a consumer ends up paying. Suppose your material costs were 5%. Multiply the material cost by 20 to calculate the selling price of your hat! How does this compare with high street prices?

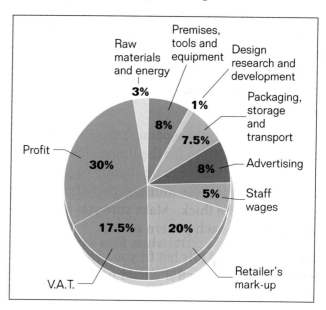

Using ICT

You will find it useful to use a spreadsheet to work out your costings. A spreadsheet makes it easy to alter the cost of one element and see the effect on the overall cost of making different batch sizes.

DESIGN SHEET 7c

• Costing

Fabric	£
Lining	£
Velcro	£
Thread	£
Label	£
Badge	£
TOTAL COST OF MATERIALS	£

All these costs are reduced when bulk buying.

On your design sheets

- Create a production specification for your hat. **7a**

- List the materials and equipment you will need. **7b**

- Prepare costings for your product. **7c**

Remember

- Detailed product specifications ensure the smooth transformation of the product from the design stage to batch production.

Indian Textile Traditions (1)

2

Next you need to learn more about traditional Indian textile techniques, designs and motifs. India is legendary for the variety and colour of its textiles.

Textile growth

The traditions of cloth manufacture and the production of handmade textiles in India continue to develop and flourish. India remains one of the most original, creative and prolific sources of textile production in the world. Its manufacturing base continues to grow.

Appliqué

You have already experienced this technique in unit 3 (see page 60). Appliqué involves stitching pieces of fabric onto a ground fabric for decorative purposes. This may have developed from the need to sew patches onto damaged cloth. Patched cloth has also been used by many religions and mystical groups as a symbol of poverty and giving up material possessions. The range of materials that can be used is enormous.

Appliqué handicrafts in Puri, India.

Reverse appliqué

Reverse appliqué is a more complicated technique. The top layer of fabric becomes the background. Shapes are stitched through both layers. Sections are then cut out of the top layer to reveal the bottom layer of fabric.

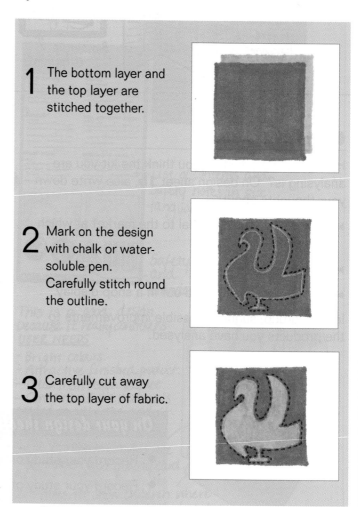

1 The bottom layer and the top layer are stitched together.

2 Mark on the design with chalk or water-soluble pen. Carefully stitch round the outline.

3 Carefully cut away the top layer of fabric.

Taking it further

1 Try creating a design using three layers of fabric.

2 Add further detail by adding extra stitches or beads.

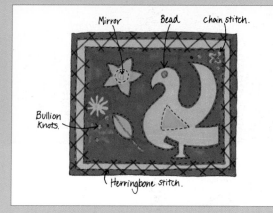

Indian quilts

Quilts from Rajasthan in the north west of India are often worked in bold floral and abstract patterns in a combination of appliqué and reverse appliqué. Sections of the top layer are cut and folded back before sewing down to create a repetitive or symmetrical design. These quilts were used as decorative soft furnishings.

● On task Apply what you know / Investigate

1. Do some test pieces to learn how to do reverse appliqué. Make a record of what you did on design sheet **2a**.

2. Working as a group, plan and carry out an investigation of Indian textiles. Record what you discover on design sheet **2b**.

On your design sheets

- Record how you did your reverse appliqué work. **2a**

- Document what you find out about Indian textiles. **2b**

Remember

- Indian textiles are very diverse in terms of colour, shapes and techniques.

- Decorative techniques such as appliqué are often a good way to recycle fabrics.

Indian Textile Traditions (2)

Kanthas are some of the most interesting Indian folk textiles. They are produced in the north east of India and also in Bangladesh. They are an early form of quilting. On these pages you will learn more about them.

Kanthas

Traditionally, kanthas were made out of cast-off saris, which were often white in colour. This was a way of 'recycling' old fabrics. Kanthas were used as bed quilts, for wrapping special things in, or for wedding guests to sit on.

To make a quilt, layers of cloth and padding are laid on top of each other and tacked together. They are then stitched together securely around the edges and at intervals across the central area. This holds the layers together and gives a padded effect.

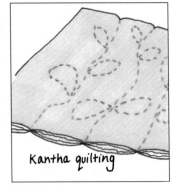

A kantha from Bengal embroided with cotton thread.

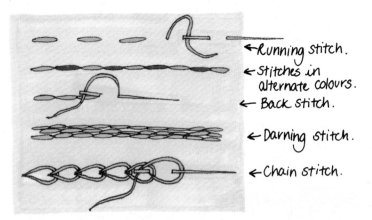

←Running stitch.

←Stitches in alternate colours.

← Back stitch.

←Darning stitch.

←Chain stitch.

Kanthas are embroidered using a simple running stitch. Indian women started to enrich the embroidery with scenes of home, nature, legend and religion. More complicated stitches were used. Areas were often outlined in chain stitch and then filled with running stitches in a different colour. Threads were taken from the coloured borders of the saris for this purpose.

By 1925, kantha making had died out due to the pressures of industrialisation. It has now been revived to cater for the tourist and export markets.

● On task 1 Investigate

What can you find out about kanthas? Record what you discover on design sheet **3a**.

Re-use it – green textiles

Kanthas, appliqué and patchwork are excellent examples of **recycling**. Families in many cultures re-used fabrics by developing these textile techniques.

● *On task 2   Have good ideas / Investigate*

1. Where could you find fabrics that could be recycled for your project? Could using recycled textiles be a feature of your design? Write your ideas down on design sheet **3b**.

2. Carry out an investigation on the **environmental impact** of textile production. Consider the different stages of textile manufacture – production of natural and synthetic fibres, dyeing and printing, finishing, product manufacture, packaging and transport. Your research could be done using the Internet. Write down your findings on design sheet **3c**.

Embroidery

Embroidery is the art of using stitches to decorate. You are already familiar with the simpler stitches such as running stitch, from unit 1 (see page 21, for example).

● *On task 3 Apply what you know*

Experiment with more complex stitches to create a series of test pieces. Add an account of your experiments to design sheet **2a** (see page 121).

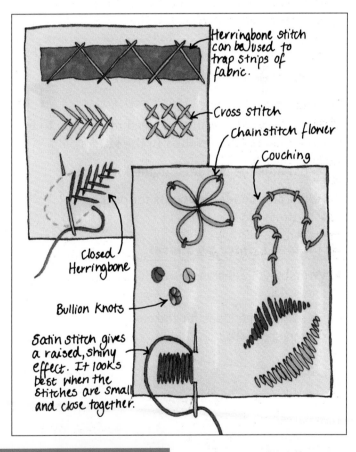

Herringbone stitch can be used to trap strips of fabric.

Cross stitch

Chainstitch flower

Couching

Closed Herringbone

Bullion Knots

Satin stitch gives a raised, shiny effect. It looks best when the stitches are small and close together.

• How I can recycle textiles at home.

1. Recycle clothes : deposit in recycling bins (contact council for nearest bin).
   : wash clothes and take them to a charity shop.

2. Tear up old textiles and use them as dusters or rags.

3. Use old fabrics for patchwork or appliqué.

4. Make presents out of textiles e.g. lavender bags, head bands or a denim pencil case from an old pair of jeans.

DESIGN SHEET 3b

On your design sheets

- Investigate Indian kanthas. **3a**
- Make notes about recycling textile products. **3b**
- Find out more about the impact of textile production on the environment. **3c**

Remember

- Kanthas are an early form of quilting.
- Several techniques can be combined in one textile piece.

What's Inside?

4

You may already have some ideas for your textile design kit and the way it will be packaged. Now you need to sketch them out so you can discuss them later with the rest of your group.

Design specification

Before you start sketching your design ideas, focus on what it is your design must do.

▷ Who is this kit for?

▷ What basic skills will users need to have already?

▷ What new skills will they need to develop to be able to make the product in the kit?

▷ What must be included in the kit?

▷ What are the requirements for packaging?

● *On task 1 Have good ideas*

1. Write up your design **specification** on design sheet **4a**.

2. **Sketch** some ideas for the contents of your kit on design sheet **4b**.

Expanding the range

You could design a kit that:

▷ used one technique to make one motif

▷ used one technique to make several different motifs

▷ used several different techniques to make one motif

▷ used several different techniques to make several different motifs.

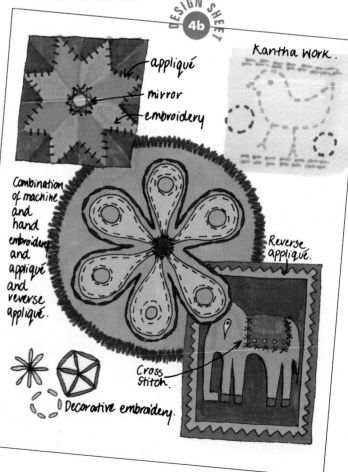

Product packaging: inside out

The way in which products are packaged is very important.

The packaging needs to provide protection for the contents in a single container. The outside of the package needs to give an idea of what is inside. It also needs to look attractive so people will want to buy it, either for themselves or to give as a present.

The package could be just a simple cardboard box, or a plastic bag. Can you design something more unusual and desirable that will make it more suitable as a gift? For example, it could include parts made from fabrics or textile-related components as decorations. However, do remember that the more complex your package design the more expensive it would be to manufacture in industry, because of added material and labour costs.

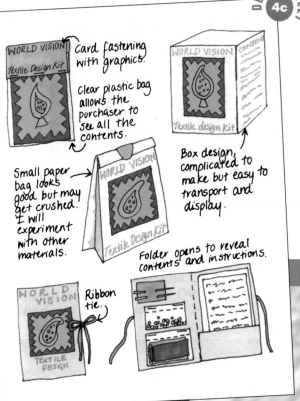

DESIGN SHEET 4c

WORLD VISION Textile Design Kit — Card fastening with graphics.

Clear plastic bag allows the purchaser to see all the contents.

WORLD VISION CONTENTS Textile design kit — Box design, complicated to make but easy to transport and display.

Small paper bag looks good but may get crushed. I will experiment with other materials.

WORLD VISION Textile Design Kit

Folder opens to reveal contents and instructions.

WORLD VISION Ribbon tie. TEXTILE DESIGN

● On task 2 Have good ideas

Sketch some designs for unusual ways to package your textile design kit. Do this on design sheet **4c**.

On your design sheets

- Write out your design specification. **4a**
- Sketch out your ideas for the kit. **4b**
- Suggest unusual methods of packaging for your kit. **4c**

Remember

- Writing a design specification will focus your mind on exactly what your customer wants.
- Produce as many ideas at this stage as possible. Keep an open mind about the possibilities.

Production Plan

Finally you need to set up your production line. You will need to work together as a team to produce a batch of products using your sampler design as quickly and efficiently as possible.

Getting organised

As before, it's essential you discuss and agree your production plan as a team. How can you arrange the tasks in order to complete the making of your products as quickly as possible? For example, two people could complete the appliqué and the other two add the embroidery. In industry, there are always elivery deadlines. The more quickly the products are made, the cheaper the labour costs, and the lower the final price.

● On task 1
Plan the making

In your group, discuss the various ways of making a batch of ten of your product as a team. Look back at page 110. Use the production process symbols to turn a list of manufacturing steps into a flow-chart for making your product.

Remember to add in quality control check points and safety procedures. One member of the team needs to be checking the whole process to make sure it is running as smoothly as possible.

Include details to show where each operation will be carried out. Use different coloured lines and symbols to work out the production route. Record your production plan flow-chart on design sheet **9a**.

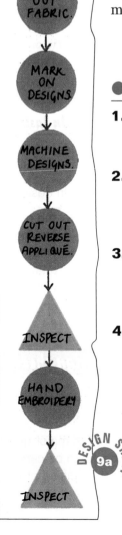

Getting in line

When all the operations have been identified, you will need to plan the layout of the production line. Where will each operation be carried out? How can the workspace be most efficiently organised?

In industry, this process is often completed on a computer. The computer can then simulate the manufacturing process to check it works.

● On task 2 Work with materials

1. Working with your team, make a batch of ten of your product. Follow your production plan closely. Time how long it takes.

2. Record the results of the quality inspections during the production process. When you stop the process, you can use this information to help identify areas that are causing problems.

3. After your team has made four of the product, stop the process. Ask everyone what problems there have been. Record what happened on design sheet **9b**.

4. Modify your plan to improve the production process.

Working well together?

Keeping the shelves stocked with the products that people want is vital. If a company can't deliver enough of a product on time, the consumer will soon start to shop elsewhere. Speeding up production time is essential.

In a traditional production line, each operator works separately and is often unaware of the finished product. The work is repetitive, and requires a low skill level, which results in low morale and a high level of rejected products.

'Quick Response Manufacture' was pioneered in the UK by Coates Viyella as a response to increasing market pressure. It involved the following:

▶ Production was reorganised in small modular units. These are more flexible and controllable and allow swift changes in response to rapid changes in the market place. If a product is not selling it can be adjusted in hours rather than days and without costly changes to factory layout.

▶ The units are based on the principles of team working. Each self-contained production unit is made up of eight operators and is arranged in a 'horse-shoe' shape. This encourages a sense of ownership.

▶ Each worker is multi-skilled and the units manage themselves to balance the workload.

▶ Quality is built into the process and observed throughout by every individual. Each finished garment is approved by a team member. Production errors are reduced and overall quality is improved.

▶ 'Piecework' which means workers get paid according to the number of products on which they work, has been abolished and each operator earns a set wage, Pressure to exceed targets is self-imposed and each team works together to earn bonuses.

▶ Production rate is higher and operators are motivated to stay longer and reach their full potential.

Final evaluation

You have already done your final evaluation of your textile design kit and the way you presented it. Now you need to evaluate your batch-production plan, and the way you worked together as a team.

● On task 3 Evaluate

Read the case-study above and the Traidcraft interview on pages 136–137. In your groups discuss the following questions.

1. How have Coates Viyella tried to motivate their workers?

2. Why are people who live in Bangladesh and Zimbabwe always keen to work for companies that export their produce through Traidcraft?

Record the conclusions of your discussion on design sheet **9c**.

● On task 4 Final evaluation

On design sheet **9d**, write up an evaluation of how well you think your team worked together to:

▶ take decisions
▶ make the final prototype
▶ deliver the presentation
▶ make a batch of your product.

On your design sheets

● Draw up a detailed production plan for your product as a flow-chart. **9a**

● Describe what happened during production. **9b**

● Record the conclusions of your discussion about the case-study. **9c**

● Write a final evaluation on the way your team worked together. **9d**

Remember

● The most efficient production systems keep everyone busy all the time.

● The quicker a product is made, the cheaper the final selling price can be.

Textiles Technology Dictionary

Aesthetics

Aesthetics is all about how people respond to things through their senses. What we see, hear, taste, touch and smell can be pleasant or distressing experiences.

Different people like and dislike different things. Generally, however, people respond well to things that are **harmonious** (go together well), or provide **contrast** (are opposites).

What makes a textile product aesthetically pleasing? Designs include elements like colour, texture and shape. It is how these elements are combined within one design that can make it appealing. A jacket can be an appealing colour but if the shape and texture is wrong it can spoil the design.

Analysis

To **analyse** a product means studying it in smaller, more detailed parts. For example, if you were to analyse a rucksack you would need to describe the material, trimmings, fastenings, how it has been constructed and how many pattern pieces have been used to make it.

Conflicting demands

Most design decisions involve making **compromises**. For example, a rucksack needs to be strong but light. Products that are strong tend to use more material. Materials and components that provide a balance between strength and weight need to be used.

Extra design features and materials that look good and last a long time are likely to increase the cost of a product. Other materials might be cheap and easy to work but could cause environmental damage.

Components

Products are usually made up of a number of smaller parts, called **components**. It is often cheaper and quicker for a manufacturer to buy in some components that they cannot produce themselves. In textiles a manufacturer making casual jackets might buy in zips, buttons, Velcro, piping, embroidered logos and so on.

Consumers

Consumers are the people who will eventually use the products you are designing. Remember that consumers have a choice. If they don't want or like what you have designed, they won't use it. The particular group of consumers your product is aimed at is sometimes called the **target market**.

As you design, keep in mind exactly what people need physically and want emotionally. Your product needs to do the job the consumer wants it to, and make them feel good about using it.

Constraints

Constraints are things that limit the possibilities of your design. For example, there may be certain sizes, weights or types of materials you cannot use, or have been told you must use.

For example, a sportswear designer is constrained by the fact that athletes need lightweight, streamlined garments. Therefore, they cannot use materials that are too heavy or create designs that are too fussy.

Design brief, proposal and specification

The **design brief** is the starting point of a project or task. It usually contains general information about what is needed, who the product is intended for and any major constraints.

The design brief is usually provided by the 'client'. This is the person who has asked you to design something for them. Your client could be from a large company, a local business, or someone you know. Make sure you know who the users of your product will be. It will probably not be the client!

A **design specification** sets out in more detail what the final product needs to do, and any other restrictions. It states any minimum and maximum sizes and weights, materials, finishes, production methods, costs, and so on.

A **design proposal** is a suggestion for a possible solution that you present to someone else for their comments. Throughout a project you are likely to need to produce several design proposals for approval by your client (or, in school, by your teacher) until you reach your final solution.

A **production specification** provides a precise description of the final product and how it should be made. It usually contains information about sizes, quantities, materials, components, methods of production, as well as quality indicators and tolerances.

Environmental impact

Everything we make has an effect on the natural **eco-system** of our planet. There is a danger that the system could become permanently damaged. There is no such thing as a completely environmentally-friendly product, but it is possible to reduce the impact and extent of the damage caused to help maintain a balance.

In textiles this may mean:

▷ making sure that dyes do not pollute the rivers

▷ limiting the amount of pesticides used when growing cotton

▷ limiting material waste and using less energy

▷ recycling or re-using textiles materials.

139

Information and communication technology (ICT)

ICT has had a major impact on the way products are designed and made. There are many opportunities in textiles to use computers. Think carefully about when it is appropriate to use them.

Computer-aided design (CAD)

There are many different types of CAD packages. Some are two-dimensional and are commonly known as drawing, paint, desk-top publishing or desk-top video programs. Others are three-dimensional, allowing the screen images to be turned and looked at from different angles. Some programs make animation in 2D or 3D easy.

Computer-aided manufacture (CAM)

Two-dimensional computer-aided designs can be printed out or saved to a disk. Data from three-dimensional designs can be sent directly to machine tools, which can produce solid objects automatically.

Control systems

Computers can be used to control sequences of events, turning circuits on and off, speeding things up or slowing them down and feeding back information from sensing devices to keep things running smoothly. Computer-aided sewing machines are controlled in this way.

Databases

Databases are collections of information (text, numbers or images) that are held or organised on a computer hard drive. A database program can search, cross-reference and present information very quickly, and can be very useful during the investigating stages of a design and technology project.

Presentation packages

These programs enable you to present information on screen. You could use one to explain to an audience the main features of your design proposal. Words and images can be animated and sound and video sequences added.

Spreadsheets

Spreadsheets help with complex calculations. Once set up, they can be used to calculate the effect of changing one element of a design on all the other parts. The data from a spreadsheet can also be displayed quickly as a graph or chart.

Word-processors

Word-processors are sophisticated typewriters that enable text to be checked and changed before being printed out. Word-processed text can be easily placed into desk-top publishing programs where it can be laid out in columns and arranged alongside to illustrations.

World Wide Web

The **Internet** provides access to information from across the world. **Search engines** can help you find what you want.

You can also design web pages of your own. Many organisations have their own websites.

Manufacturing

There are a number of ways that products can be made:

▷ **One-off** production is where a single item is made on its own.

▷ **Batch-production** is where a specific number of items are made together, saving time and materials. The **production**, or **cell**, line can then be quickly changed to make a batch of a different design.

▷ **Mass-production** is where identical products are made all the time. The different stages are sometimes carried out by different people, working on a conveyor-belt system.

As you develop your final design idea you will need to consider how it can be made as a one-off item in school and in quantity.

Modelling ideas

Making new products takes a lot of time, effort and money, so it's a good idea to trial your designs as much possible so that mistakes can be avoided.

To discover if something will work you don't necessarily have to make it the same size as the real thing, or use the same materials. Drawings, diagrams, samples, prototypes and test and trial pieces are all quicker and cheaper to create than the real thing.

Think carefully about what you want to learn about your design from your samples. Decide which is the best sort of model to make to get the information you need.

In your textiles work you might model a product in paper or scrap material. You might try out details of your product, such as making a pocket, or experiment with techniques such as appliqué.

Patterns

Flat patterns are paper **templates** used when making textile products. They are standard shapes used for cutting identical pieces. For example, using the same flat pattern allows you to cut out fifty size 14 T-shirts, which will be exactly the same size and shape.

A **pattern** can also be a repeated shape or motif used to create a fabric design.

Presentation

The way you present your design and technology work is very important. The sequence of sheets (or design folder) you hand in during or at the end of a project needs to clearly show the process you have used to investigate, develop, plan and evaluate your design ideas.

Remember that your design folder helps provide important evidence that you have achieved your targets. Good presentation won't cover up poor thinking, but evidence of good thinking can easily get lost if the presentation is poor.

In industry, designers must think carefully about how they present their ideas. They must compete with other designers and a good presentation is more likely to impress a client than a careless one.

Properties and characteristics of materials

Different materials behave in different ways. They are said to have different physical and chemical properties. Fabrics have different **properties** and **characteristics** because they are required to suit many different end-uses. For example, cotton fabrics crease easily and are difficult to iron when dry, whereas polyester fabrics are more crease-resistant and easier to iron. Mixing these fibres in one fabric results in a fabric with positive properties of both.

Production drawings

Production drawings are more like diagrams. It should be possible for someone else (a machinist, for example) to make up the design from your drawing.

Unlike sketches, production drawings need to be very neat and accurate, and do not use colour.

Samples

In industry, **samples** of new designs are always made. This allows the client to see it before a final decision is made about producing it. This prevents the wrong product design arriving in the shops and saves a lot of time and money if no-one wants to buy it.

Sometimes many samples are made up in different sizes and using different materials before it is 'right'.

A sample garment may be worn by someone to see how well it performs in wear and how well it washes. The threads, stitches and trimmings to be used, and the quickest way to produce a product in quantity, can also be worked out from a sample.

Sometimes a sample is modelled first in cheap fabric such as calico. This is called a **toile**. This happens more often with expensive garments.

Sketches

Sketches are particular types of drawings used to record information and explore ideas. They should not be drawn very neatly using a ruler: this takes too long – they need to be quick so you can move on rapidly. Sketches often include notes or labels to help explain the ideas or to record passing thoughts. In textiles, they usually include colour.

Smart materials

When some materials are processed or combined in a particular way their behaviour can change. New **smart materials** can change their properties and characteristics in response to changes in temperature, humidity or electrical charge.

The textiles industry

They are two major parts to the textile industry.

The first produces materials that can be woven, knitted, printed or dyed. The second produces clothes and products made from textiles. Textile materials are manufactured and then ordered and bought in by manufacturers of clothing and other products.

When considering how your design would be made in industry, it is important to realise that textile materials will be bought in. They will not be printed or dyed in the same factory where the products will be made.

Index